Shamrock & Spoon: Modern Irish Cooking for Every Occasion

S.R. Moore

Published by S.R. Moore, 2024.

SHAMROCK & SPOON: MODERN IRISH COOKING FOR EVERY OCCASION

First edition. February 24, 2024.

Copyright © 2024 S.R. Moore.

ISBN: 979-8224760558

Written by S.R. Moore.

Table of Contents

Introduction

Welcome to "Shamrock & Spoon: Modern Irish Cooking for Every Occasion," a culinary journey through the vibrant and diverse flavors of Ireland, reimagined for the modern palate. In this cookbook, we invite you to elevate your St. Patrick's Day celebrations and beyond with contemporary twists on classic Irish dishes, meticulously crafted to delight and inspire.

Irish cuisine is steeped in tradition, with hearty stews, comforting potato dishes, and rich, indulgent treats woven into the fabric of its culinary heritage. At "Shamrock & Spoon," we pay homage to these timeless favorites while infusing them with creativity, innovation, and a touch of gourmet flair.

Whether you're hosting a festive gathering with friends and family or simply craving a taste of Ireland's culinary delights, our cookbook has something for every occasion. From Guinness-infused stews that simmer with depth and richness to whiskey-glazed salmon that dazzles the senses, each recipe has been thoughtfully curated to showcase the best of Irish cooking in a contemporary light.

But "Shamrock & Spoon" is more than just a collection of recipes; it's a celebration of Irish culture, hospitality, and the joy of sharing delicious food with loved ones. Throughout these pages, you'll find not only mouthwatering dishes but also stories, tips, and culinary insights that capture the essence of Ireland's culinary landscape.

Join us as we explore the intersection of tradition and innovation, where time-honored recipes meet modern techniques, and where every meal is an opportunity to create lasting memories. Whether you're a seasoned home cook or a culinary enthusiast eager to explore new flavors, "Shamrock & Spoon" promises to be your trusted companion on a culinary journey through the Emerald Isle.

So raise a glass to good food, good company, and the spirit of St. Patrick's Day, and let "Shamrock & Spoon" guide you on a gastronomic adventure that celebrates the rich tapestry of Irish cuisine in all its glory. Sláinte!

Appetizers

1. Guinness and Cheddar Dip with Pretzel Bites

2. Smoked Salmon Crostini with Dill Cream Cheese

3. Boxty Potato Pancakes with Sour Cream and Chives

4. Irish Whiskey Glazed Meatballs

5. Dublin Bay Prawn Cocktail with Homemade Marie Rose Sauce

Guinness and Cheddar Dip with Pretzel Bites

Ingredients:
For the dip:
- 1 cup Guinness stout
- 8 oz cream cheese, softened
- 2 cups sharp cheddar cheese, shredded
- 1/4 cup sour cream
- 2 cloves garlic, minced
- 1 teaspoon Worcestershire sauce
- 1/2 teaspoon smoked paprika
- Salt and pepper to taste
- Chopped chives or green onions, for garnish

For the pretzel bites:
- 1 lb pizza dough, homemade or store-bought
- 4 cups water
- 1/4 cup baking soda
- Coarse sea salt or pretzel salt, for sprinkling
- Melted butter, for brushing (optional)

Instructions:
For the dip:
1. In a small saucepan, bring the Guinness stout to a simmer over medium heat. Cook until it reduces by half, about 10-15 minutes. Remove from heat and let it cool slightly.
2. In a mixing bowl, combine the softened cream cheese, shredded cheddar cheese, sour cream, minced garlic, Worcestershire sauce, smoked paprika, salt, and pepper. Mix until well combined.
3. Gradually add the reduced Guinness stout to the cheese mixture, stirring until smooth and creamy.
4. Transfer the dip to a serving bowl and garnish with chopped chives or green onions.

For the pretzel bites:
1. Preheat your oven to 425°F (220°C). Line a baking sheet with parchment paper.
2. Divide the pizza dough into small pieces and roll each piece into a ball, about 1-inch in diameter.
3. In a large pot, bring the water and baking soda to a boil. Drop the dough balls into the boiling water, a few at a time, and boil for about 30 seconds. Remove them with a slotted spoon and place them on the prepared baking sheet.
4. Sprinkle the boiled dough balls with coarse sea salt or pretzel salt.
5. Bake the pretzel bites in the preheated oven for 12-15 minutes, or until golden brown and crispy.
6. Optional: Brush the baked pretzel bites with melted butter for extra flavor.
7. Serve the Guinness and Cheddar Dip with the warm pretzel bites for dipping.

Tips and Variations:

- **Beer Selection:** Feel free to use your favorite stout or dark beer in place of Guinness for different flavor variations.

- **Cheese Options:** Experiment with different types of cheese such as Irish cheddar, smoked Gouda, or Dubliner cheese for unique flavor profiles.

- **Dip Enhancements:** Add crispy cooked bacon bits, diced jalapeños, or chopped sun-dried tomatoes to the dip for extra flavor and texture.

- **Homemade Pretzel Dough:** If you prefer, you can make your own pretzel dough from scratch using a homemade recipe.

- **Make-Ahead:** Both the dip and the pretzel bites can be prepared in advance and reheated just before serving. Store any leftovers in the refrigerator and reheat them in the oven or microwave.

- **Customization:** Serve the dip with other dippers such as sliced vegetables, crackers, or toasted bread for variety.

Smoked Salmon Crostini with Dill Cream Cheese

Ingredients:
For the dill cream cheese:
- 8 oz cream cheese, softened
- 2 tablespoons fresh dill, chopped
- 1 tablespoon lemon juice
- Zest of 1 lemon
- Salt and pepper to taste

For the crostini:
- 1 French baguette, sliced into 1/2-inch thick rounds
- 2 tablespoons olive oil
- 4 oz smoked salmon, thinly sliced
- 2 tablespoons capers, drained
- Fresh dill sprigs, for garnish

Instructions:
For the dill cream cheese:
1. In a mixing bowl, combine the softened cream cheese, chopped fresh dill, lemon juice, lemon zest, salt, and pepper. Mix until well combined and smooth. Taste and adjust seasoning if needed.
2. Cover the bowl and refrigerate the dill cream cheese until ready to use.

For the crostini:
1. Preheat your oven to 375°F (190°C). Arrange the baguette slices in a single layer on a baking sheet.
2. Brush the tops of the baguette slices with olive oil.
3. Bake in the preheated oven for 8-10 minutes, or until the crostini are golden and crispy. Remove from the oven and let them cool slightly.

Assembly:
1. Spread a generous amount of dill cream cheese onto each crostini.
2. Top each crostini with a slice of smoked salmon.
3. Garnish each crostini with a few capers and a sprig of fresh dill.
4. Arrange the Smoked Salmon Crostini with Dill Cream Cheese on a serving platter and serve immediately.

Tips and Variations:

- **Cream Cheese Options:** If you prefer a lighter option, you can use Greek yogurt or whipped cream cheese instead of regular cream cheese for the dill spread.

- **Bread Alternatives:** If French baguette is not available, you can use sliced sourdough bread, ciabatta, or even crackers as the base for the crostini.

- **Flavor Enhancements:** Add a touch of sweetness to the crostini by drizzling them with honey or balsamic glaze before serving.

- **Customization:** Feel free to add additional toppings to the crostini, such as sliced cucumber, avocado, or red onion, for extra flavor and texture.

- **Make-Ahead:** You can prepare the dill cream cheese and bake the crostini in advance. Assemble the crostini with smoked salmon just before serving to keep them fresh and crispy.

- **Wine Pairing:** Serve the Smoked Salmon Crostini with a crisp white wine such as Sauvignon Blanc or Chardonnay for a perfect pairing.

Boxty Potato Pancakes with Sour Cream and Chives

Ingredients:
For the boxty potato pancakes:
- 2 cups grated raw potatoes
- 2 cups mashed potatoes
- 1 cup all-purpose flour
- 1 teaspoon baking powder
- 1 teaspoon salt
- 1/2 teaspoon black pepper
- 1/2 cup milk
- 2 eggs, lightly beaten
- 2 tablespoons unsalted butter, melted
- 2 tablespoons chopped fresh chives
- Vegetable oil, for frying

For the sour cream and chive topping:
- 1 cup sour cream
- 2 tablespoons chopped fresh chives
- Salt and pepper to taste

Instructions:

For the boxty potato pancakes:

1. In a large mixing bowl, combine the grated raw potatoes, mashed potatoes, all-

purpose flour, baking powder, salt, and black pepper.

2. In a separate bowl, whisk together the milk, eggs, and melted butter.

3. Pour the wet ingredients into the dry ingredients and stir until well combined. Fold in the chopped fresh chives.

4. Heat a large skillet or griddle over medium heat and lightly grease it with vegetable oil.

5. Drop spoonfuls of the boxty batter onto the skillet, spreading them out slightly with the back of a spoon to form pancakes. Cook for 3-4 minutes on each side, or until golden brown and cooked through.

6. Transfer the cooked boxty potato pancakes to a plate lined with paper towels to drain excess oil.

For the sour cream and chive topping:

1. In a small bowl, mix together the sour cream and chopped fresh chives. Season with salt and pepper to taste.

Assembly:

1. Serve the warm boxty potato pancakes immediately, topped with a dollop of sour cream and chive mixture.

2. Garnish with additional chopped chives, if desired.

3. Enjoy the Boxty Potato Pancakes with Sour Cream and Chives as a delicious appetizer or side dish for your St. Patrick's Day celebration!

Tips and Variations:

- **Additions:** Feel free to add grated cheese, diced cooked bacon, or chopped scallions to the boxty batter for extra flavor and texture.

- **Make-Ahead:** You can prepare the boxty batter in advance and store it in the refrigerator until ready to cook. Simply give it a quick stir before cooking the pancakes.

- **Dipping Sauces:** Serve the boxty potato pancakes with additional dipping sauces such as apple sauce, horseradish cream, or caramelized onion dip for extra flavor options.

- **Vegan Option:** Substitute non-dairy milk and vegan butter for the dairy ingredients to make this recipe vegan-friendly. Serve the pancakes with a dairy-free sour cream alternative.

- **Gluten-Free:** Use a gluten-free flour blend in place of all-purpose flour to make this recipe gluten-free.

Irish Whiskey Glazed Meatballs

Ingredients:

For the meatballs:
- 1 lb ground beef
- 1/2 cup breadcrumbs
- 1/4 cup grated Parmesan cheese
- 1 egg
- 2 cloves garlic, minced
- 2 tablespoons fresh parsley, chopped
- 1 teaspoon dried thyme
- Salt and pepper to taste
- Olive oil, for cooking

For the Irish whiskey glaze:
- 1/4 cup Irish whiskey
- 1/4 cup brown sugar
- 1/4 cup ketchup
- 2 tablespoons apple cider vinegar
- 1 tablespoon Worcestershire sauce
- 1 teaspoon Dijon mustard
- Salt and pepper to taste
- Chopped fresh parsley, for garnish (optional)

Instructions:

For the meatballs:

1. Preheat your oven to 400°F (200°C). Line a baking sheet with parchment paper.

2. In a large mixing bowl, combine the ground beef, breadcrumbs, grated Parmesan cheese, egg, minced garlic, chopped parsley, dried thyme, salt, and pepper. Mix until well combined.

3. Shape the mixture into meatballs, about 1-inch in diameter, and place them on the prepared baking sheet.

4. Drizzle the meatballs with olive oil and bake in the preheated oven for 15-20 minutes, or until cooked through and browned on the outside.

For the Irish whiskey glaze:

1. In a small saucepan, combine the Irish whiskey, brown sugar, ketchup, apple cider vinegar, Worcestershire sauce, Dijon mustard, salt, and pepper.

2. Bring the mixture to a simmer over medium heat, stirring occasionally.

3. Reduce the heat to low and let the glaze simmer for 5-7 minutes, or until it thickens slightly.

4. Remove the glaze from the heat and set aside.

Assembly:

1. Once the meatballs are cooked, transfer them to a large skillet over medium heat.

2. Pour the Irish whiskey glaze over the meatballs in the skillet, stirring gently to coat them evenly.

3. Allow the meatballs to simmer in the glaze for 2-3 minutes, or until the glaze thickens and coats the meatballs.

4. Garnish the Irish Whiskey Glazed Meatballs with chopped fresh parsley, if desired.

5. Serve the meatballs immediately as a delicious appetizer or main dish for your St. Patrick's Day celebration!

Tips and Variations:

- **Meat Options:** Feel free to use ground pork, ground turkey, or a mixture of meats in place of ground beef for variety.

- **Gluten-Free Option:** Use gluten-free breadcrumbs or crushed gluten-free crackers in place of regular breadcrumbs to make this recipe gluten-free.

- **Vegetarian Option:** Substitute cooked lentils or chickpeas for the ground meat to make vegetarian meatballs, and adjust the cooking time as needed.

- **Make-Ahead:** You can prepare the meatballs and the glaze in advance and store them separately in the refrigerator. Simply reheat the meatballs and glaze on the stove before serving.

- **Serve with Sides:** Pair the Irish Whiskey Glazed Meatballs with mashed potatoes, roasted vegetables, or a fresh salad for a complete meal.

Dublin Bay Prawn Cocktail with Homemade Marie Rose Sauce

Ingredients:
For the prawn cocktail:
- 1 lb Dublin Bay prawns (or large shrimp), cooked and peeled
- 4 cups mixed salad greens
- 1 avocado, diced
- 1/2 English cucumber, diced
- 1 lemon, cut into wedges
- Fresh dill sprigs, for garnish

For the homemade Marie Rose sauce:
- 1/2 cup mayonnaise
- 2 tablespoons ketchup
- 1 tablespoon lemon juice
- 1 teaspoon Worcestershire sauce
- 1 teaspoon Dijon mustard
- 1/2 teaspoon paprika
- Salt and pepper to taste
- Dash of hot sauce (optional)

Instructions:

For the homemade Marie Rose sauce:

1. In a small bowl, whisk together the mayonnaise, ketchup, lemon juice, Worcestershire sauce, Dijon mustard, paprika, salt, pepper, and hot sauce (if using). Adjust seasoning to taste.

2. Cover the bowl and refrigerate the Marie Rose sauce until ready to use.

For the prawn cocktail:

1. In a large mixing bowl, combine the cooked and peeled Dublin Bay prawns with diced avocado and cucumber.

2. Divide the mixed salad greens among serving glasses or bowls.

3. Spoon the prawn mixture on top of the salad greens in each glass or bowl.

4. Squeeze fresh lemon juice over the prawns and garnish with fresh dill sprigs.

5. Serve the Dublin Bay Prawn Cocktail with Homemade Marie Rose Sauce on the side for dipping or drizzle it over the prawns before serving.

Tips and Variations:

- **Prawn Alternatives:** If Dublin Bay prawns are not available, you can use large shrimp or even cooked lobster meat for a luxurious twist.

- **Greens Variation:** Feel free to use your favorite salad greens such as arugula, butter lettuce, or baby spinach in place of mixed salad greens.

- **Additional Ingredients:** Enhance the prawn cocktail with additional ingredients such as diced mango, cherry tomatoes, or sliced radishes for extra flavor and texture.

- **Make-Ahead:** Prepare the prawn mixture and Marie Rose sauce in advance and store them separately in the refrigerator. Assemble the prawn cocktail just before serving to keep the ingredients fresh and crisp.

- **Presentation:** Serve the Dublin Bay Prawn Cocktail in elegant cocktail glasses or martini glasses for a sophisticated presentation.

- **Side Suggestions:** Accompany the prawn cocktail with crusty bread, Irish soda bread, or buttered toast points for a delicious contrast in texture.

Soups and Salads

1. Potato Leek Soup with Crispy Shallots

2. Traditional Irish Stew with Soda Bread Croutons

3. Watercress and Pear Salad with Cashel Blue Cheese

4. Smoked Haddock Chowder

5. Warm Kale Salad with Roasted Butternut Squash and Pomegranate Seeds

Potato Leek Soup with Crispy Shallots

Ingredients:

For the soup:
- 4 leeks, white and light green parts only, thinly sliced
- 4 large potatoes, peeled and diced
- 4 cups vegetable or chicken broth
- 2 cups water
- 1 cup heavy cream
- 2 tablespoons butter
- Salt and pepper to taste
- Fresh chives, finely chopped, for garnish

For the crispy shallots:
- 4 shallots, thinly sliced
- 1/2 cup all-purpose flour
- Vegetable oil for frying
- Salt to taste

Instructions:

For the soup:

1. In a large pot, melt the butter over medium heat. Add the sliced leeks and cook until softened, about 5-7 minutes.

2. Add the diced potatoes to the pot, along with the vegetable or chicken broth and water. Bring to a boil, then reduce the heat to low and simmer for about 15-20 minutes, or until the potatoes are tender.

3. Using an immersion blender or transferring the mixture to a blender in batches, puree the soup until smooth.

4. Stir in the heavy cream and season with salt and pepper to taste. Allow the soup to simmer for an additional 5 minutes to heat through.

5. Meanwhile, prepare the crispy shallots.

For the crispy shallots:

1. In a shallow dish, season the flour with salt. Dredge the thinly sliced shallots in the seasoned flour, shaking off any excess.

2. In a large skillet, heat vegetable oil over medium-high heat. Once the oil is hot, add the dredged shallots in batches, frying until golden and crispy, about 2-3 minutes per batch. Use a slotted spoon to transfer the crispy shallots to a paper towel-lined plate to drain excess oil.

Assembly:

1. Ladle the hot Potato Leek Soup into bowls.

2. Top each bowl with a generous spoonful of crispy shallots and a sprinkle of fresh chives.

3. Serve the Potato Leek Soup with Crispy Shallots immediately, accompanied by crusty bread or Irish soda bread if desired.

Tips and Variations:

- **Vegetarian Option:** Use vegetable broth instead of chicken broth to make this soup vegetarian-friendly.

- **Make it Vegan:** Substitute the heavy cream with coconut cream or a non-dairy alternative for a vegan version of this soup.

- **Texture Variation:** For a chunkier soup, reserve some of the cooked potatoes before pureeing and stir them back into the soup after blending.

- **Flavor Enhancements:** Add a pinch of nutmeg or a dash of smoked paprika to the soup for added depth of flavor.

- **Make-Ahead:** The soup can be made in advance and reheated just before serving. Store the crispy shallots separately to maintain their crispiness.

- **Garnish Ideas:** Experiment with different garnishes such as grated cheese, crumbled bacon, or a drizzle of truffle oil for additional flavor and visual appeal.

Traditional Irish Stew with Soda Bread Croutons

Ingredients:
For the Irish Stew:
- 2 lbs lamb shoulder, cut into bite-sized pieces
- 3 tablespoons olive oil
- 4 carrots, peeled and sliced
- 4 celery stalks, sliced
- 2 onions, chopped
- 4 cloves garlic, minced
- 4 cups beef or vegetable broth
- 1 cup Guinness stout
- 4 large potatoes, peeled and diced
- 2 tablespoons tomato paste
- 2 bay leaves
- 2 teaspoons fresh thyme leaves
- Salt and pepper to taste
- Chopped fresh parsley, for garnish

For the Soda Bread Croutons:
- 4 slices Irish soda bread, cut into cubes
- 2 tablespoons olive oil
- Salt and pepper to taste

Instructions:

For the Irish Stew:

1. In a large Dutch oven or heavy-bottomed pot, heat 2 tablespoons of olive oil over medium-high heat. Season the lamb pieces with salt and pepper, then brown them in batches until they are evenly browned on all sides. Remove the lamb from the pot and set aside.

2. Add the remaining tablespoon of olive oil to the pot. Add the carrots, celery, onions, and garlic, and sauté until the vegetables are softened, about 5-7 minutes.

3. Return the browned lamb to the pot. Add the beef or vegetable broth, Guinness stout, diced potatoes, tomato paste, bay leaves, and thyme leaves. Stir to combine.

4. Bring the stew to a boil, then reduce the heat to low and let it simmer, partially covered, for about 1 1/2 to 2 hours, or until the lamb is tender and the flavors have melded together. Season with additional salt and pepper to taste.

For the Soda Bread Croutons:

1. Preheat your oven to 375°F (190°C). Line a baking sheet with parchment paper.

2. Place the cubed Irish soda bread on the prepared baking sheet. Drizzle with olive oil and season with salt and pepper. Toss to coat the bread cubes evenly.

3. Bake in the preheated oven for 10-12 minutes, or until the croutons are golden and crispy.

Assembly:

1. Ladle the hot Irish stew into bowls.

2. Top each bowl of stew with a handful of soda bread croutons.

3. Garnish with chopped fresh parsley.

4. Serve the Traditional Irish Stew with Soda Bread Croutons immediately, accompanied by additional slices of Irish soda bread or crusty bread for dipping.

Tips and Variations:

- **Meat Substitution:** If you prefer, you can use beef instead of lamb for the stew. Choose a well-marbled cut such as chuck or stewing beef for best results.

- **Vegetarian Option:** Omit the meat altogether and make a hearty vegetarian Irish stew using a variety of root vegetables such as parsnips, turnips, and rutabagas.

- **Slow Cooker Method:** This stew can also be made in a slow cooker for added convenience. Simply brown the meat and sauté the vegetables as instructed, then transfer everything to the slow cooker and cook on low for 6-8 hours or on high for 3-4 hours.

- **Flavor Enhancements:** Add a splash of Worcestershire sauce or balsamic vinegar to the stew for an extra depth of flavor.

- **Leftover Love:** This stew tastes even better the next day, so don't hesitate to make a big batch and enjoy the leftovers for lunch or dinner throughout the week.

- **Customize Your Croutons:** Experiment with different seasonings for the soda bread croutons, such as garlic powder, dried herbs, or grated Parmesan cheese.

Watercress and Pear Salad with Cashel Blue Cheese

Ingredients:

For the salad:
- 6 cups watercress, tough stems removed
- 2 ripe pears, thinly sliced
- 1/2 cup candied walnuts or pecans
- 1/4 cup dried cranberries or pomegranate seeds
- 1/4 cup thinly sliced red onion

For the dressing:
- 1/4 cup extra virgin olive oil
- 2 tablespoons white wine vinegar
- 1 tablespoon honey
- 1 teaspoon Dijon mustard
- Salt and pepper to taste

For the Cashel Blue Cheese:
- 4 oz Cashel Blue cheese, crumbled

Instructions:

1. In a large salad bowl, combine the watercress, sliced pears, candied walnuts or pecans, dried cranberries or pomegranate seeds, and sliced red onion.

2. In a small bowl, whisk together the extra virgin olive oil, white wine vinegar, honey, Dijon mustard, salt, and pepper to make the dressing.

3. Drizzle the dressing over the salad and toss gently to coat all the ingredients evenly.

4. Top the salad with crumbled Cashel Blue cheese.

5. Serve the Watercress and Pear Salad with Cashel Blue Cheese immediately as a refreshing and elegant starter or side dish.

Tips and Variations:

- **Variety of Greens:** If watercress is not available, you can use baby spinach, arugula, or mixed salad greens instead.

- **Pear Selection:** Choose ripe but firm pears for the salad to add a natural sweetness and crisp texture. Varieties such as Anjou or Bartlett work well.

- **Nut Options:** Feel free to substitute the candied walnuts or pecans with toasted almonds or hazelnuts for a different flavor and texture.

- **Dried Fruit Alternatives:** If dried cranberries or pomegranate seeds are not to your liking, you can use sliced fresh strawberries, raspberries, or apple slices for a burst of freshness.

- **Cheese Substitutions:** If Cashel Blue cheese is not available, you can use another creamy blue cheese such as Roquefort, Gorgonzola, or Stilton.

- **Make-Ahead:** You can prepare the dressing and salad ingredients ahead of time and assemble the salad just before serving to keep the greens crisp and fresh.

- **Enhanced Flavor:** For an extra burst of flavor, you can add a drizzle of balsamic glaze or sprinkle of freshly ground black pepper over the assembled salad.

Smoked Haddock Chowder

Ingredients:
- 1 lb smoked haddock fillets, skin removed
- 4 slices thick-cut bacon, diced
- 1 large onion, diced
- 2 cloves garlic, minced
- 2 stalks celery, diced
- 2 carrots, diced
- 2 medium potatoes, peeled and diced
- 4 cups fish or vegetable broth
- 1 cup whole milk
- 1 cup heavy cream
- 2 tablespoons all-purpose flour
- 2 tablespoons butter
- 1 bay leaf
- 1 teaspoon fresh thyme leaves
- Salt and pepper to taste
- Chopped fresh parsley, for garnish
- Crusty bread or Irish soda bread, for serving

Instructions:

1. In a large pot, cook the diced bacon over medium heat until crispy. Remove the bacon from the pot and set it aside, leaving the bacon fat in the pot.

2. Add the diced onion, minced garlic, celery, and carrots to the pot. Sauté for 5-7 minutes, or until the vegetables are softened.

3. Stir in the diced potatoes and cook for another 2-3 minutes.

4. Add the butter to the pot and allow it to melt. Sprinkle the flour over the vegetables and stir to coat.

5. Slowly pour in the fish or vegetable broth, stirring constantly to prevent lumps from forming. Add the bay leaf and fresh thyme leaves.

6. Bring the chowder to a simmer and let it cook for 15-20 minutes, or until the potatoes are tender.

7. While the chowder is simmering, prepare the smoked haddock. Cut the smoked haddock into bite-sized pieces.

8. Add the smoked haddock pieces to the chowder and cook for an additional 5 minutes, or until the fish is cooked through.

9. Stir in the whole milk and heavy cream. Season with salt and pepper to taste.

10. Remove the bay leaf from the chowder. Ladle the smoked haddock chowder into bowls and garnish with the crispy bacon pieces and chopped fresh parsley.

11. Serve the Smoked Haddock Chowder immediately, accompanied by crusty bread or Irish soda bread for dipping.

Tips and Variations:

- **Seafood Variation:** If smoked haddock is not available, you can use other smoked fish such as salmon or trout for a different flavor profile.

- **Creamy Texture:** For an even creamier chowder, you can blend a portion of the cooked vegetables with the broth before adding the fish and cream.

- **Vegetarian Option:** Omit the bacon and use vegetable broth instead of fish broth for a vegetarian version of this chowder. You can also add extra vegetables such as corn or peas for added flavor and texture.

- **Spice it Up:** Add a pinch of cayenne pepper or a dash of hot sauce for a bit of heat, if desired.

- **Make-Ahead:** This chowder tastes even better the next day, so feel free to make it ahead of time and reheat it gently on the stove before serving.

Warm Kale Salad with Roasted Butternut Squash and Pomegranate Seeds

Ingredients:
For the salad:
- 1 medium butternut squash, peeled, seeded, and diced
- 2 tablespoons olive oil
- Salt and pepper to taste
- 1 bunch kale, stems removed and leaves torn into bite-sized pieces
- 1/4 cup pomegranate seeds
- 1/4 cup crumbled feta cheese or goat cheese
- 1/4 cup chopped walnuts or pecans, toasted
- 1 tablespoon balsamic vinegar (optional)

For the dressing:
- 2 tablespoons extra virgin olive oil
- 1 tablespoon maple syrup or honey
- 1 tablespoon Dijon mustard
- 1 tablespoon apple cider vinegar
- Salt and pepper to taste

Instructions:

1. Preheat your oven to 400°F (200°C). Place the diced butternut squash on a baking sheet, drizzle with olive oil, and season with salt and pepper. Toss to coat evenly. Roast in the preheated oven for 20-25 minutes, or until the squash is tender and caramelized.

2. While the butternut squash is roasting, prepare the kale. In a large mixing bowl, massage the torn kale leaves with a drizzle of olive oil and a pinch of salt for a few minutes until the kale is tenderized.

3. In a small bowl, whisk together the ingredients for the dressing: extra virgin olive oil, maple syrup or honey, Dijon mustard, apple cider vinegar, salt, and pepper.

4. Once the butternut squash is done roasting, allow it to cool slightly. Add the roasted butternut squash, pomegranate seeds, crumbled feta or goat cheese, and chopped toasted walnuts or pecans to the bowl with the massaged kale.

5. Drizzle the dressing over the salad and toss gently to combine all the ingredients.

6. Serve the Warm Kale Salad with Roasted Butternut Squash and Pomegranate Seeds immediately, garnished with an extra sprinkle of pomegranate seeds and crumbled cheese if desired. Optionally, add a splash of balsamic vinegar for extra flavor.

Tips and Variations:

- **Greens Variation:** If kale is not your preference, you can use baby spinach or Swiss chard instead for a different flavor and texture.

- **Seed Alternatives:** If pomegranate seeds are not available, you can use dried cranberries or golden raisins for a sweet and tart contrast.

- **Cheese Options:** Experiment with different types of cheese such as blue cheese, Gouda, or Parmesan for a unique flavor profile.

- **Nutty Crunch:** Feel free to use any type of nuts you prefer, such as almonds, pine nuts, or sunflower seeds, for added texture and crunch.

- **Make-Ahead:** You can roast the butternut squash and prepare the dressing ahead of time, then assemble the salad just before serving to keep the kale fresh and vibrant.

- **Customization:** Add grilled chicken, shrimp, or tofu to make this salad a complete meal.

Brunch Favorites

1. Irish Breakfast Hash with Fried Eggs

2. Smoked Salmon and Scrambled Eggs on Soda Bread

3. Boxty Benedict with Irish Bacon and Hollandaise Sauce

4. Potato and Chive Frittata

5. Oatmeal Pancakes with Whiskey Maple Syrup

Irish Breakfast Hash with Fried Eggs

Ingredients:
- 4 slices bacon, diced
- 1 onion, diced
- 2 cloves garlic, minced
- 2 large potatoes, diced into small cubes
- 1 cup cooked corned beef, diced
- 1 bell pepper, diced
- 1 teaspoon smoked paprika
- Salt and pepper to taste
- 4 large eggs
- Chopped fresh parsley or chives, for garnish

Instructions:

1. In a large skillet, cook the diced bacon over medium heat until crispy. Remove the bacon from the skillet and set it aside, leaving the bacon fat in the skillet.

2. Add the diced onion to the skillet and sauté until translucent, about 5 minutes. Add the minced garlic and cook for an additional minute.

3. Add the diced potatoes to the skillet, spreading them out in an even layer. Let them cook without stirring for a few minutes to allow them to brown on one side.

4. Stir the potatoes and continue to cook until they are golden brown and cooked through, about 10-12 minutes.

5. Add the diced corned beef and diced bell pepper to the skillet. Sprinkle with smoked paprika, salt, and pepper. Stir to combine all the ingredients.

6. Cook for an additional 5-7 minutes, or until the corned beef is heated through and the bell pepper is tender.

7. While the hash is cooking, fry the eggs in a separate skillet to your desired doneness.

8. Divide the Irish Breakfast Hash among serving plates. Top each portion with a fried egg.

9. Garnish with the crispy bacon pieces and chopped fresh parsley or chives.

10. Serve the Irish Breakfast Hash with Fried Eggs immediately, accompanied by toast or Irish soda bread if desired.

Tips and Variations:

- **Vegetarian Option:** Omit the bacon and corned beef to make this dish vegetarian-friendly. You can add extra vegetables such as mushrooms, spinach, or cherry tomatoes for added flavor and texture.

- **Meat Variation:** Instead of corned beef, you can use cooked sausage, ham, or even leftover roast beef for a different twist on this dish.

- **Spice it Up:** Add a dash of hot sauce or sprinkle of crushed red pepper flakes for a bit of heat, if desired.

- **Cheese Topping:** Sprinkle grated cheddar cheese or crumbled feta cheese over the hash just before serving for extra richness and flavor.

- **Customization:** Feel free to customize the hash with your favorite ingredients such as diced tomatoes, green onions, or cooked beans for added variety.

- **Make-Ahead:** You can prepare the hash ingredients in advance and store them in the refrigerator. Simply reheat them in a skillet before serving and fry the eggs fresh.

Smoked Salmon and Scrambled Eggs on Soda Bread

Ingredients:

For the soda bread:
- 2 cups all-purpose flour
- 1 teaspoon baking soda
- 1 teaspoon salt
- 1 cup buttermilk
- 1 tablespoon honey
- 1 tablespoon unsalted butter, melted
- 1 tablespoon chopped fresh dill (optional)

For the scrambled eggs:
- 6 large eggs
- 1/4 cup milk or cream
- Salt and pepper to taste
- 1 tablespoon unsalted butter
- 4 oz smoked salmon, sliced
- Fresh dill sprigs, for garnish

Instructions:
For the soda bread:
1. Preheat your oven to 375°F (190°C). Grease a baking sheet or line it with parchment paper.
2. In a large mixing bowl, whisk together the all-purpose flour, baking soda, and salt.
3. In a separate bowl, combine the buttermilk, honey, and melted butter.
4. Gradually add the wet ingredients to the dry ingredients, stirring until a dough forms. Fold in the chopped fresh dill, if using.
5. Turn the dough out onto a floured surface and shape it into a round loaf.
6. Place the loaf onto the prepared baking sheet. Use a sharp knife to score a deep cross into the top of the loaf.
7. Bake in the preheated oven for 35-40 minutes, or until the bread is golden brown and sounds hollow when tapped on the bottom.
8. Remove the soda bread from the oven and let it cool on a wire rack.

For the scrambled eggs:
1. In a mixing bowl, whisk together the eggs, milk or cream, salt, and pepper until well combined.
2. Heat a skillet over medium heat and melt the butter. Pour the egg mixture into the skillet.
3. Gently scramble the eggs with a spatula, stirring occasionally, until they are cooked to your desired consistency.
4. Once the scrambled eggs are cooked, remove them from the heat and set aside.

Assembly:
1. Slice the soda bread into thick slices and toast them lightly.
2. Place a generous portion of scrambled eggs on each slice of toasted soda bread.

3. Top the scrambled eggs with slices of smoked salmon.

4. Garnish each slice with fresh dill sprigs.

5. Serve the Smoked Salmon and Scrambled Eggs on Soda Bread immediately as a delicious and satisfying breakfast or brunch option for St. Patrick's Day.

Tips and Variations:

- **Creamy Eggs:** For extra creamy scrambled eggs, you can add a dollop of cream cheese or crème fraîche to the egg mixture before cooking.

- **Herb Variations:** Feel free to use other fresh herbs such as chives, parsley, or tarragon in place of dill for different flavor profiles.

- **Serving Suggestions:** Accompany the Smoked Salmon and Scrambled Eggs on Soda Bread with a side of sliced tomatoes, avocado, or a mixed green salad for a complete meal.

- **Vegetarian Option:** Omit the smoked salmon and serve the scrambled eggs with sautéed spinach, roasted mushrooms, or grilled tomatoes for a vegetarian-friendly version of this dish.

- **Make-Ahead:** You can prepare the soda bread dough in advance and bake it just before serving. Leftover soda bread can be stored in an airtight container for 2-3 days and reheated before serving.

Boxty Benedict with Irish Bacon and Hollandaise Sauce

Ingredients:
For the boxty pancakes:
- 2 cups grated raw potatoes
- 1 cup mashed potatoes
- 1 cup all-purpose flour
- 1 teaspoon baking powder
- 1 teaspoon salt
- 1/2 cup milk
- 2 tablespoons unsalted butter, melted
- 4 large eggs

For the Hollandaise sauce:
- 3 large egg yolks
- 1 tablespoon lemon juice
- 1/2 cup unsalted butter, melted
- Pinch of cayenne pepper
- Salt to taste

For assembling:
- 8 slices Irish bacon or Canadian bacon
- 4 large eggs
- Chopped fresh chives or parsley, for garnish

Instructions:

For the boxty pancakes:

1. In a large mixing bowl, combine the grated raw potatoes, mashed potatoes, all-purpose flour, baking powder, salt, milk, melted butter, and eggs. Mix until well combined.

2. Heat a large skillet or griddle over medium heat and lightly grease it with butter or oil.

3. Pour 1/4 cup of the boxty batter onto the skillet for each pancake. Spread the batter into a round shape with the back of a spoon.

4. Cook the boxty pancakes for 3-4 minutes on each side, or until golden brown and cooked through. Remove from the skillet and keep warm.

For the Hollandaise sauce:

1. Fill a saucepan with a few inches of water and bring it to a simmer over medium heat.

2. In a heatproof bowl that fits snugly over the saucepan, whisk together the egg yolks and lemon juice until pale and thickened.

3. Place the bowl over the saucepan of simmering water (make sure the bottom of the bowl doesn't touch the water).

4. Slowly drizzle in the melted butter, whisking constantly, until the sauce thickens and emulsifies.

5. Remove the bowl from the heat and stir in a pinch of cayenne pepper and salt to taste. Keep the Hollandaise sauce warm until ready to serve.

For assembling:

1. In a separate skillet, cook the Irish bacon or Canadian bacon until crispy. Remove from the skillet and keep warm.

2. Poach the eggs in simmering water for 3-4 minutes, or until the whites are set but the yolks are still runny.

3. To assemble each Boxty Benedict, place two boxty pancakes on a serving plate. Top each pancake with a slice of crispy bacon, followed by a poached egg.

4. Drizzle the Hollandaise sauce over the poached eggs.

5. Garnish with chopped fresh chives or parsley.

6. Serve the Boxty Benedict with Irish Bacon and Hollandaise Sauce immediately, accompanied by a side of roasted tomatoes or sautéed spinach, if desired.

Tips and Variations:

- **Vegetarian Option:** Substitute the Irish bacon with sliced avocado or sautéed mushrooms for a vegetarian-friendly version of this dish.

- **Smoked Salmon Variation:** For a luxurious twist, replace the Irish bacon with smoked salmon slices.

- **Herb Variation:** Add chopped fresh herbs such as dill or tarragon to the Hollandaise sauce for extra flavor.

- **Make-Ahead:** You can prepare the boxty pancakes and Hollandaise sauce in advance and reheat them gently before assembling the Boxty Benedict.

- **Customization:** Feel free to customize the toppings by adding sliced tomatoes, wilted spinach, or caramelized onions for extra flavor and texture.

Potato and Chive Frittata

Ingredients:
- 8 large eggs
- 1/4 cup milk or cream
- Salt and pepper to taste
- 2 tablespoons olive oil
- 1 small onion, diced
- 2 cloves garlic, minced
- 2 medium potatoes, peeled and thinly sliced
- 1/2 cup grated Irish cheddar cheese
- 2 tablespoons chopped fresh chives
- Optional: 1/4 cup cooked diced bacon or ham

Instructions:

1. Preheat your oven to 350°F (175°C).

2. In a large mixing bowl, whisk together the eggs, milk or cream, salt, and pepper until well combined. Set aside.

3. Heat the olive oil in a large oven-safe skillet over medium heat. Add the diced onion and garlic, and sauté until softened and fragrant, about 3-4 minutes.

4. Add the thinly sliced potatoes to the skillet and cook, stirring occasionally, until they are tender and lightly golden brown, about 8-10 minutes.

5. If using, sprinkle the cooked diced bacon or ham over the potatoes in the skillet.

6. Pour the egg mixture evenly over the potatoes and onions in the skillet. Sprinkle the grated Irish cheddar cheese and chopped fresh chives on top.

7. Cook the frittata on the stovetop for 3-4 minutes, or until the edges start to set.

8. Transfer the skillet to the preheated oven and bake the frittata for 12-15 minutes, or until the eggs are set and the top is golden brown.

9. Remove the frittata from the oven and let it cool slightly before slicing.

10. Slice the Potato and Chive Frittata into wedges and serve warm.

Tips and Variations:

- **Vegetarian Option:** Omit the bacon or ham for a vegetarian version of this frittata. You can add extra vegetables such as bell peppers, spinach, or mushrooms for added flavor and nutrition.

- **Cheese Options:** Feel free to use your favorite cheese in place of Irish cheddar. Gruyère, feta, or goat cheese would all work well in this recipe.

- **Herb Variation:** Experiment with different herbs such as parsley, basil, or thyme for different flavor profiles.

- **Make-Ahead:** You can prepare the Potato and Chive Frittata in advance and store it in the refrigerator. Reheat individual slices in the microwave or enjoy them cold as a grab-and-go breakfast option.

- **Serving Suggestions:** Serve the frittata with a side salad, crusty bread, or roasted vegetables for a complete meal. It's also delicious with a dollop of sour cream or salsa on top.

Oatmeal Pancakes with Whiskey Maple Syrup

Ingredients:

For the oatmeal pancakes:
- 1 cup old-fashioned oats
- 1 cup buttermilk
- 1 cup all-purpose flour
- 2 tablespoons brown sugar
- 1 teaspoon baking powder
- 1/2 teaspoon baking soda
- 1/2 teaspoon salt
- 2 large eggs
- 1/4 cup unsalted butter, melted
- 1 teaspoon vanilla extract

For the whiskey maple syrup:
- 1 cup pure maple syrup
- 2 tablespoons Irish whiskey
- 1 teaspoon vanilla extract

Instructions:

For the oatmeal pancakes:

1. In a large mixing bowl, combine the old-fashioned oats and buttermilk. Let the mixture soak for 10-15 minutes.

2. In a separate bowl, whisk together the all-purpose flour, brown sugar, baking powder, baking soda, and salt.

3. After the oats have soaked, add the eggs, melted butter, and vanilla extract to the oat mixture. Stir until well combined.

4. Gradually add the dry ingredients to the wet ingredients, stirring until just combined. Do not overmix; the batter should be slightly lumpy.

5. Heat a lightly greased skillet or griddle over medium heat. Pour 1/4 cup of batter onto the skillet for each pancake.

6. Cook the pancakes for 2-3 minutes on each side, or until golden brown and cooked through.

7. Transfer the cooked pancakes to a plate and keep them warm while you prepare the whiskey maple syrup.

For the whiskey maple syrup:

1. In a small saucepan, combine the pure maple syrup, Irish whiskey, and vanilla extract.

2. Bring the mixture to a simmer over medium heat, stirring occasionally.

3. Reduce the heat to low and let the syrup simmer for 5-7 minutes, or until it thickens slightly.

4. Remove the syrup from the heat and let it cool for a few minutes before serving.

Assembly:

1. Stack the oatmeal pancakes on serving plates.

2. Drizzle the warm whiskey maple syrup over the pancakes.

3. Serve the Oatmeal Pancakes with Whiskey Maple Syrup immediately, accompanied by fresh fruit, whipped cream, or additional butter if desired.

Tips and Variations:

- **Additions:** Feel free to add extras to the oatmeal pancake batter, such as chopped nuts, dried fruit, or chocolate chips, for extra flavor and texture.

- **Gluten-Free Option:** You can use gluten-free oats and a gluten-free all-purpose flour blend to make this recipe gluten-free.

- **Make-Ahead:** Prepare the pancake batter and whiskey maple syrup in advance and store them separately in the refrigerator. Simply reheat the pancakes in the toaster or microwave and warm the syrup on the stove before serving.

- **Flavor Variations:** Experiment with different types of whiskey or flavored syrups to create unique variations of this recipe. You can also add a pinch of cinnamon or nutmeg to the syrup for extra warmth and spice.

Main Courses

1. Guinness Beef Stew with Colcannon Mash

2. Whiskey Glazed Salmon with Champ

3. Shepherd's Pie with Sweet Potato Topping

4. Bangers and Mash with Onion Gravy

5. Dublin Coddle with Crusty Bread

Guinness Beef Stew with Colcannon Mash

Ingredients:
For the Guinness Beef Stew:
- 2 lbs stewing beef, cut into bite-sized pieces
- Salt and pepper to taste
- 2 tablespoons all-purpose flour
- 2 tablespoons olive oil
- 1 large onion, diced
- 2 cloves garlic, minced
- 4 carrots, peeled and sliced
- 4 celery stalks, sliced
- 2 tablespoons tomato paste
- 2 cups beef broth
- 1 (14.9 oz) can Guinness Stout
- 2 bay leaves
- 1 teaspoon dried thyme
- 1 teaspoon paprika
- 1 tablespoon Worcestershire sauce
- 2 tablespoons chopped fresh parsley, for garnish

For the Colcannon Mash:
- 2 lbs potatoes, peeled and diced
- 4 tablespoons unsalted butter
- 1 cup milk or cream
- 1 small head cabbage, finely shredded
- 4 green onions, finely chopped
- Salt and pepper to taste

Instructions:

For the Guinness Beef Stew:

1. Season the stewing beef with salt and pepper, then toss it in flour to coat evenly.

2. Heat olive oil in a large pot or Dutch oven over medium-high heat. Brown the beef in batches, ensuring not to overcrowd the pot. Remove the beef and set it aside.

3. In the same pot, add diced onion and minced garlic. Sauté until softened, about 5 minutes.

4. Add sliced carrots and celery to the pot and cook for another 5 minutes.

5. Stir in tomato paste and cook for 1-2 minutes.

6. Return the browned beef to the pot. Pour in beef broth and Guinness Stout. Add bay leaves, dried thyme, paprika, and Worcestershire sauce.

7. Bring the stew to a boil, then reduce the heat to low and let it simmer, covered, for 1.5 to 2 hours, or until the beef is tender and the flavors have melded together.

8. Taste and adjust seasoning with salt and pepper if needed.

For the Colcannon Mash:

1. Boil the diced potatoes in salted water until tender, about 15-20 minutes. Drain well.

2. In a separate pot, melt butter over medium heat. Add shredded cabbage and chopped green onions. Sauté until the cabbage is wilted and softened, about 5-7 minutes.

3. Add the cooked potatoes to the pot with the cabbage mixture. Mash them until smooth and creamy, adding milk or cream as needed to achieve the desired consistency.

4. Season the Colcannon Mash with salt and pepper to taste.

Assembly:

1. Ladle the Guinness Beef Stew into bowls.

2. Serve the stew alongside generous scoops of Colcannon Mash.

3. Garnish with chopped fresh parsley before serving.

4. Enjoy your elevated Guinness Beef Stew with Colcannon Mash as a hearty and comforting meal for St. Patrick's Day!

Tips and Variations:

- **Vegetarian Option:** Substitute the stewing beef with diced mushrooms or root vegetables like parsnips and turnips for a vegetarian version of this dish.

- **Slow Cooker Method:** You can also prepare the Guinness Beef Stew in a slow cooker. Simply brown the beef and sauté the vegetables as instructed, then transfer everything to a slow cooker and cook on low for 6-8 hours or on high for 3-4 hours.

- **Beer Alternatives:** If Guinness Stout is not available, you can use another stout or dark beer with rich flavor.

- **Make-Ahead:** Both the Guinness Beef Stew and Colcannon Mash can be made ahead of time and reheated before serving. This makes it a convenient option for entertaining guests on St. Patrick's Day!

Whiskey Glazed Salmon with Champ

Ingredients:
For the whiskey glazed salmon:
- 4 salmon fillets (about 6 oz each)
- Salt and pepper to taste
- 1/4 cup Irish whiskey
- 2 tablespoons brown sugar
- 2 tablespoons soy sauce
- 2 cloves garlic, minced
- 1 teaspoon grated fresh ginger
- 1 tablespoon olive oil
- Chopped fresh parsley or green onions, for garnish

For the champ:
- 2 lbs potatoes, peeled and quartered
- 1/2 cup milk
- 4 tablespoons unsalted butter
- 4 green onions, finely chopped
- Salt and pepper to taste

Instructions:
For the whiskey glazed salmon:
1. Season the salmon fillets with salt and pepper to taste. Set aside.
2. In a small bowl, whisk together the Irish whiskey, brown sugar, soy sauce, minced garlic, and grated ginger to make the glaze.
3. Heat olive oil in a skillet over medium-high heat. Place the salmon fillets in the skillet, skin side down, and cook for 3-4 minutes, or until the skin is crispy and browned.
4. Flip the salmon fillets and pour the whiskey glaze over them. Cook for another 3-4 minutes, basting the salmon with the glaze, until the salmon is cooked through and glazed.
5. Remove the salmon from the skillet and let it rest for a few minutes.

For the champ:
1. Place the peeled and quartered potatoes in a large pot of salted water. Bring to a boil and cook until the potatoes are fork-tender, about 15-20 minutes.
2. While the potatoes are cooking, heat the milk and butter in a small saucepan over low heat until the butter is melted.
3. Drain the cooked potatoes and return them to the pot. Mash the potatoes until smooth.
4. Gradually pour the warm milk and butter mixture into the mashed potatoes, stirring until the champ reaches the desired consistency. You may not need to use all of the milk and butter.
5. Stir in the finely chopped green onions and season the champ with salt and pepper to taste.

Assembly:
1. Spoon the champ onto serving plates.
2. Place a whiskey glazed salmon fillet on top of each serving of champ.
3. Drizzle any remaining whiskey glaze over the salmon fillets.
4. Garnish with chopped fresh parsley or green onions.

5. Serve the Whiskey Glazed Salmon with Champ immediately as a delicious and elegant main dish for your St. Patrick's Day celebration!

Tips and Variations:
- **Alternative Fish:** If you prefer, you can use other types of fish such as trout or cod for this recipe.

- **Glaze Variation:** Experiment with different glazes by adding ingredients like honey, mustard, or maple syrup for extra flavor.

- **Vegetarian Option:** Substitute the salmon with grilled or roasted portobello mushrooms for a vegetarian-friendly version of this dish.

- **Side Suggestions:** Serve the Whiskey Glazed Salmon with Champ alongside roasted vegetables, sautéed greens, or a fresh salad for a complete meal.

- **Make-Ahead:** You can prepare the whiskey glaze and champ in advance and store them separately in the refrigerator. Simply reheat the glaze and champ before serving with freshly cooked salmon.

Shepherd's Pie with Sweet Potato Topping

Ingredients:
For the filling:
- 1 tablespoon olive oil
- 1 large onion, diced
- 2 carrots, diced
- 2 cloves garlic, minced
- 1 lb ground lamb or beef
- 1 tablespoon tomato paste
- 1 tablespoon Worcestershire sauce
- 1 cup frozen peas
- 1 cup beef or vegetable broth
- 1 tablespoon cornstarch (optional, for thickening)
- Salt and pepper to taste
- Chopped fresh parsley, for garnish

For the sweet potato topping:
- 2 large sweet potatoes, peeled and cubed
- 2 tablespoons unsalted butter
- 1/4 cup milk or cream
- Salt and pepper to taste
- Pinch of nutmeg (optional)

Instructions:
For the filling:
1. Preheat your oven to 375°F (190°C).
2. Heat olive oil in a large skillet over medium heat. Add diced onion and carrots, and cook until softened, about 5 minutes.
3. Add minced garlic and cook for an additional minute.
4. Add ground lamb or beef to the skillet, breaking it up with a spoon. Cook until browned and cooked through.
5. Stir in tomato paste and Worcestershire sauce, and cook for 1-2 minutes.
6. Add frozen peas and beef or vegetable broth to the skillet. If desired, mix cornstarch with a tablespoon of water to create a slurry and add it to the skillet to thicken the filling. Cook for another 5 minutes, or until the filling is thickened. Season with salt and pepper to taste.

For the sweet potato topping:
1. Place the cubed sweet potatoes in a pot of salted water. Bring to a boil and cook until the sweet potatoes are fork-tender, about 15 minutes.
2. Drain the cooked sweet potatoes and return them to the pot.
3. Add butter and milk or cream to the pot with the sweet potatoes. Mash until smooth and creamy. Season with salt, pepper, and nutmeg (if using).

Assembly:
1. Transfer the filling to a baking dish and spread it out evenly.
2. Spoon the mashed sweet potatoes over the filling, spreading them out to cover the filling completely.
3. Use a fork to create a decorative pattern on the surface of the sweet potatoes.
4. Place the baking dish in the preheated oven and bake for 25-30 minutes, or until the filling is bubbling and the sweet potato topping is golden brown.

5. Remove from the oven and let it cool for a few minutes before serving.

6. Garnish with chopped fresh parsley before serving.

7. Serve the Shepherd's Pie with Sweet Potato Topping warm as a comforting and hearty dish for your St. Patrick's Day celebration!

Tips and Variations:

- **Vegetarian Option:** Substitute the ground lamb or beef with lentils or mushrooms for a vegetarian version of this dish.

- **Cheese Topping:** Sprinkle grated cheddar cheese over the sweet potato topping before baking for added flavor and richness.

- **Herb Variation:** Add chopped fresh herbs such as rosemary, thyme, or sage to the filling for extra flavor.

- **Make-Ahead:** You can assemble the Shepherd's Pie in advance and store it in the refrigerator. Simply bake it when ready to serve for a convenient meal option.

- **Side Suggestions:** Serve the Shepherd's Pie with a side of steamed green beans, roasted Brussels sprouts, or a mixed green salad for a balanced meal.

Bangers and Mash with Onion Gravy

Ingredients:
For the bangers:
- 8 pork sausages
- 2 tablespoons olive oil

For the mashed potatoes:
- 2 lbs potatoes, peeled and cut into chunks
- 4 tablespoons unsalted butter
- 1/2 cup milk or cream
- Salt and pepper to taste

For the onion gravy:
- 2 tablespoons unsalted butter
- 2 large onions, thinly sliced
- 2 cloves garlic, minced
- 2 tablespoons all-purpose flour
- 2 cups beef or chicken broth
- 1 tablespoon Worcestershire sauce
- Salt and pepper to taste
- Chopped fresh parsley, for garnish

Instructions:

For the bangers:

1. Heat olive oil in a large skillet over medium heat. Add the pork sausages and cook until browned on all sides and cooked through, about 12-15 minutes. Remove from the skillet and set aside.

For the mashed potatoes:

1. Place the peeled and chopped potatoes in a large pot of salted water. Bring to a boil and cook until the potatoes are fork-tender, about 15-20 minutes.

2. Drain the cooked potatoes and return them to the pot.

3. Add butter and milk or cream to the pot with the potatoes. Mash until smooth and creamy. Season with salt and pepper to taste.

For the onion gravy:

1. In the same skillet used for cooking the sausages, melt butter over medium heat. Add thinly sliced onions and cook until softened and caramelized, about 15-20 minutes.

2. Add minced garlic to the skillet and cook for an additional minute.

3. Sprinkle flour over the onions and garlic, and stir to combine. Cook for 1-2 minutes to cook out the raw flour taste.

4. Gradually pour in beef or chicken broth, stirring constantly to prevent lumps from forming. Bring the mixture to a simmer and cook until the gravy thickens, about 5-7 minutes.

5. Stir in Worcestershire sauce and season with salt and pepper to taste.

Assembly:

1. Serve the mashed potatoes on serving plates.

2. Place the cooked pork sausages on top of the mashed potatoes.

3. Pour the onion gravy over the sausages and mashed potatoes.

4. Garnish with chopped fresh parsley before serving.

5. Serve the Bangers and Mash with Onion Gravy immediately as a comforting and hearty dish for your St. Patrick's Day celebration!

Tips and Variations:
- **Vegetarian Option:** Substitute the pork sausages with vegetarian or vegan sausages for a meat-free version of this dish.

- **Herb Variation:** Add chopped fresh herbs such as thyme, rosemary, or sage to the mashed potatoes for extra flavor.

- **Beer Gravy:** For an extra Irish twist, you can deglaze the skillet with a splash of Irish stout or beer before adding the broth to the onion gravy.

- **Make-Ahead:** You can prepare the mashed potatoes and onion gravy in advance and reheat them before serving. Cook the sausages just before serving for the best taste and texture.

- **Side Suggestions:** Serve the Bangers and Mash with Onion Gravy alongside steamed peas, roasted carrots, or a side salad for a complete meal.

Dublin Coddle with Crusty Bread

Ingredients:
For the Dublin Coddle:
- 8 slices thick-cut bacon, chopped
- 8 pork sausages
- 2 large onions, thinly sliced
- 4 cloves garlic, minced
- 4 large potatoes, peeled and thickly sliced
- 2 large carrots, peeled and thickly sliced
- 2 cups chicken or vegetable broth
- 1/4 cup chopped fresh parsley
- Salt and pepper to taste

For the Crusty Bread:
- 1 loaf crusty bread (such as French baguette or sourdough), sliced
- 4 tablespoons unsalted butter, melted
- 2 cloves garlic, minced
- 2 tablespoons chopped fresh parsley

Instructions:

For the Dublin Coddle:

1. Preheat your oven to 350°F (175°C).

2. In a large oven-safe pot or Dutch oven, cook the chopped bacon over medium heat until it starts to brown and render its fat, about 5 minutes.

3. Add the pork sausages to the pot and brown them on all sides, about 5 minutes. Remove the bacon and sausages from the pot and set them aside.

4. In the same pot, add the thinly sliced onions and minced garlic. Sauté until the onions are softened and translucent, about 5 minutes.

5. Layer the sliced potatoes and carrots on top of the onions in the pot. Season with salt and pepper to taste.

6. Place the cooked bacon and sausages on top of the vegetables in the pot.

7. Pour the chicken or vegetable broth over the ingredients in the pot, ensuring that everything is evenly covered.

8. Cover the pot with a lid and transfer it to the preheated oven. Bake for 1 to 1.5 hours, or until the vegetables are tender and the flavors have melded together.

9. Remove the pot from the oven and sprinkle chopped fresh parsley over the Dublin Coddle before serving.

For the Crusty Bread:

1. In a small bowl, combine melted butter, minced garlic, and chopped fresh parsley.

2. Brush the sliced crusty bread with the garlic parsley butter mixture.

3. Place the bread slices on a baking sheet and toast them in the oven at 350°F (175°C) for 5-7 minutes, or until golden brown and crispy.

Assembly:

1. Serve the Dublin Coddle hot, straight from the pot.

2. Serve the crusty bread slices alongside the Dublin Coddle for dipping and soaking up the flavorful broth.

3. Enjoy your modern twist on a classic Irish dish, perfect for celebrating St. Patrick's Day with family and friends!

Tips and Variations:

- **Vegetarian Option:** Omit the bacon and sausages, and add extra vegetables such as mushrooms, bell peppers, or parsnips for a vegetarian version of this dish.

- **Herb Variation:** Experiment with different herbs such as thyme, rosemary, or bay leaves for added flavor in the Dublin Coddle.

- **Make-Ahead:** You can prepare the Dublin Coddle in advance and reheat it before serving. The flavors will continue to develop, making it even more delicious!

- **Side Suggestions:** Serve the Dublin Coddle with a side salad, pickles, or coleslaw for a complete meal.

Vegetarian/Vegan Options

1. Mushroom and Guinness Pie with Flaky Pastry

2. Lentil Shepherd's Pie with Cauliflower Mash

3. Vegan Irish Stew with Seitan and Root Vegetables

4. Spinach and Feta Boxty Pancakes with Herb Butter

5. Roasted Vegetable and Barley Risotto with Parmesan Crisps

Mushroom and Guinness Pie with Flaky Pastry

Ingredients:
For the filling:
- 2 tablespoons olive oil
- 1 large onion, diced
- 3 cloves garlic, minced
- 1 lb mushrooms (such as button or cremini), sliced
- 2 carrots, diced
- 2 celery stalks, diced
- 2 tablespoons all-purpose flour
- 1 cup Guinness Stout
- 1 cup vegetable broth
- 2 tablespoons tomato paste
- 1 tablespoon Worcestershire sauce
- 1 teaspoon dried thyme
- Salt and pepper to taste
- 1/4 cup chopped fresh parsley

For the flaky pastry:
- 2 cups all-purpose flour
- 1/2 teaspoon salt
- 3/4 cup unsalted butter, chilled and cubed
- 1/2 cup cold water

Instructions:

For the filling:

1. Heat olive oil in a large skillet over medium heat. Add diced onion and minced garlic, and cook until softened, about 5 minutes.

2. Add sliced mushrooms to the skillet and cook until they release their moisture and start to brown, about 8-10 minutes.

3. Stir in diced carrots and celery, and cook for another 5 minutes.

4. Sprinkle all-purpose flour over the vegetables in the skillet, and stir to coat evenly.

5. Pour in Guinness Stout and vegetable broth, and stir until well combined.

6. Add tomato paste, Worcestershire sauce, and dried thyme to the skillet. Season with salt and pepper to taste.

7. Bring the mixture to a simmer and cook until the sauce thickens, about 10-15 minutes.

8. Stir in chopped fresh parsley, then remove the skillet from heat and let the filling cool slightly.

For the flaky pastry:

1. In a large mixing bowl, combine all-purpose flour and salt.

2. Add chilled and cubed butter to the flour mixture. Using a pastry blender or your fingers, cut the butter into the flour until the mixture resembles coarse crumbs.

3. Gradually add cold water to the flour mixture, mixing until the dough comes together. Be careful not to overwork the dough.

4. Shape the dough into a disc, wrap it in plastic wrap, and refrigerate for at least 30 minutes.

Assembly:

1. Preheat your oven to 375°F (190°C).

2. Roll out the chilled flaky pastry on a lightly floured surface to fit the size of your pie dish.

3. Transfer the cooled mushroom and Guinness filling to a pie dish.

4. Place the rolled-out flaky pastry over the filling in the pie dish, and crimp the edges to seal. Cut a few slits in the pastry to allow steam to escape during baking.

5. Brush the top of the pastry with an egg wash (1 beaten egg mixed with a tablespoon of water) for a golden finish.

6. Place the pie dish on a baking sheet (to catch any drips), and bake in the preheated oven for 30-35 minutes, or until the pastry is golden brown and the filling is bubbling.

7. Remove the Mushroom and Guinness Pie with Flaky Pastry from the oven and let it cool for a few minutes before serving.

8. Serve the pie warm as a hearty and flavorful main dish for your St. Patrick's Day celebration!

Tips and Variations:

- **Vegetarian Option:** Omit the Worcestershire sauce or use a vegetarian alternative to make this dish vegetarian-friendly. You can also add extra vegetables such as peas or bell peppers for added flavor and texture.

- **Meat Addition:** Feel free to add cooked diced chicken or beef to the filling for a meatier version of this pie.

- **Cheese Topping:** Sprinkle grated cheddar cheese or crumbled blue cheese over the filling before adding the pastry for extra richness and flavor.

- **Make-Ahead:** You can prepare the filling and pastry dough in advance and assemble the pie just before baking. This makes it a convenient option for entertaining guests on St. Patrick's Day!

- **Side Suggestions:** Serve the Mushroom and Guinness Pie with Flaky Pastry alongside a side salad, steamed vegetables, or mashed potatoes for a complete meal.

Lentil Shepherd's Pie with Cauliflower Mash

Ingredients:
For the lentil filling:
- 1 cup green or brown lentils, rinsed and drained
- 2 cups vegetable broth
- 2 tablespoons olive oil
- 1 large onion, diced
- 2 carrots, diced
- 2 celery stalks, diced
- 3 cloves garlic, minced
- 1 teaspoon dried thyme
- 1 teaspoon dried rosemary
- 1 tablespoon tomato paste
- 1 tablespoon soy sauce or tamari
- Salt and pepper to taste
- 1 cup frozen peas
- 1 tablespoon cornstarch (optional, for thickening)

For the cauliflower mash:
- 1 large head cauliflower, cut into florets
- 2 tablespoons unsalted butter
- 1/4 cup milk or cream
- Salt and pepper to taste

Instructions:

For the lentil filling:

1. In a medium saucepan, combine the rinsed lentils and vegetable broth. Bring to a boil, then reduce the heat to low and simmer, covered, for 20-25 minutes, or until the lentils are tender but not mushy. Drain any excess liquid and set aside.

2. Preheat your oven to 375°F (190°C).

3. In a large skillet, heat olive oil over medium heat. Add diced onion, carrots, and celery, and sauté until softened, about 5-7 minutes.

4. Add minced garlic, dried thyme, and dried rosemary to the skillet, and cook for an additional minute until fragrant.

5. Stir in tomato paste and soy sauce, and cook for another minute.

6. Add the cooked lentils to the skillet, along with salt and pepper to taste. If the mixture seems too dry, you can add a splash of vegetable broth or water. Stir in frozen peas.

7. If desired, mix cornstarch with a tablespoon of water to create a slurry, and add it to the skillet to thicken the filling. Cook for another 2-3 minutes until the filling is thickened. Remove from heat and set aside.

For the cauliflower mash:

1. Place cauliflower florets in a large pot of salted water. Bring to a boil and cook until the cauliflower is very tender, about 10-12 minutes.

2. Drain the cooked cauliflower and return it to the pot.

3. Add butter and milk or cream to the pot with the cauliflower. Use a potato masher or immersion blender to mash the cauliflower until smooth and creamy. Season with salt and pepper to taste.

Assembly:

1. Transfer the lentil filling to a baking dish and spread it out evenly.

2. Spoon the cauliflower mash over the lentil filling, spreading it out to cover the filling completely.

3. Use a fork to create a decorative pattern on the surface of the cauliflower mash.

4. Place the baking dish in the preheated oven and bake for 25-30 minutes, or until the filling is bubbly and the cauliflower mash is golden brown on top.

5. Remove from the oven and let it cool for a few minutes before serving.

6. Serve the Lentil Shepherd's Pie with Cauliflower Mash warm as a comforting and hearty dish for your St. Patrick's Day celebration!

Tips and Variations:

- **Vegetarian and Vegan Options:** This recipe is naturally vegetarian and can be made vegan by using plant-based milk and butter for the cauliflower mash.

- **Gluten-Free Option:** Ensure that the soy sauce or tamari you use is gluten-free to make this dish suitable for those with gluten sensitivities.

- **Make-Ahead:** You can prepare the lentil filling and cauliflower mash in advance and assemble the pie just before baking. This makes it a convenient option for entertaining guests on St. Patrick's Day!

- **Side Suggestions:** Serve the Lentil Shepherd's Pie with Cauliflower Mash alongside a side salad, steamed greens, or roasted vegetables for a complete meal.

Vegan Irish Stew with Seitan and Root Vegetables

Ingredients:
- 2 tablespoons olive oil
- 1 large onion, diced
- 3 cloves garlic, minced
- 2 carrots, peeled and chopped
- 2 parsnips, peeled and chopped
- 2 celery stalks, chopped
- 2 cups chopped potatoes
- 1 cup chopped turnips
- 1 cup chopped rutabaga
- 1 cup chopped seitan (or other vegan meat substitute)
- 4 cups vegetable broth
- 2 tablespoons tomato paste
- 2 bay leaves
- 1 teaspoon dried thyme
- Salt and pepper to taste
- Chopped fresh parsley, for garnish

Instructions:

1. Heat olive oil in a large pot over medium heat. Add diced onion and minced garlic, and sauté until softened, about 5 minutes.

2. Add chopped carrots, parsnips, celery, potatoes, turnips, and rutabaga to the pot. Cook for another 5 minutes, stirring occasionally.

3. Stir in chopped seitan and cook for 2-3 minutes.

4. Pour vegetable broth into the pot, ensuring that all vegetables and seitan are covered. Add tomato paste, bay leaves, dried thyme, salt, and pepper.

5. Bring the stew to a boil, then reduce the heat to low and let it simmer, covered, for 30-40 minutes, or until the vegetables are tender and the flavors have melded together.

6. Taste and adjust seasoning with salt and pepper if needed.

7. Remove the bay leaves from the stew before serving.

8. Ladle the Vegan Irish Stew with Seitan and Root Vegetables into bowls, garnish with chopped fresh parsley, and serve hot.

Tips and Variations:

- **Gluten-Free Option:** Ensure that the seitan or vegan meat substitute you use is gluten-free to make this stew suitable for those with gluten sensitivities. You can also use chickpeas or lentils instead of seitan for a gluten-free option.

- **Herb Variation:** Feel free to add other herbs such as rosemary or sage for extra flavor.

- **Make-Ahead:** This stew can be prepared in advance and reheated before serving. In fact, the flavors tend to develop even more if made ahead.

- **Side Suggestions:** Serve the Vegan Irish Stew with Seitan and Root Vegetables alongside crusty bread, Irish soda bread, or a simple green salad for a complete meal.

Spinach and Feta Boxty Pancakes with Herb Butter

Ingredients:
For the boxty pancakes:
- 1 cup grated potatoes
- 1 cup all-purpose flour
- 1 teaspoon baking powder
- 1/2 teaspoon salt
- 1/4 teaspoon black pepper
- 1/2 cup milk
- 1 egg
- 1 cup fresh spinach, finely chopped
- 1/2 cup crumbled feta cheese
- 2 tablespoons olive oil (for cooking)

For the herb butter:
- 4 tablespoons unsalted butter, softened
- 2 tablespoons chopped fresh herbs (such as parsley, chives, and dill)
- 1 clove garlic, minced
- Salt and pepper to taste

Instructions:

For the boxty pancakes:

1. In a large bowl, mix together grated potatoes, all-purpose flour, baking powder, salt, and black pepper.

2. In a separate bowl, whisk together milk and egg until well combined.

3. Pour the milk and egg mixture into the bowl with the dry ingredients, and stir until just combined.

4. Gently fold in chopped spinach and crumbled feta cheese until evenly distributed throughout the batter.

5. Heat olive oil in a large skillet or frying pan over medium heat.

6. Scoop about 1/4 cup of the batter onto the skillet for each pancake, spreading it out slightly with the back of a spoon to form a circle.

7. Cook the pancakes for 2-3 minutes on each side, or until golden brown and cooked through.

8. Remove the pancakes from the skillet and keep warm while you prepare the herb butter.

For the herb butter:

1. In a small bowl, mix together softened butter, chopped fresh herbs, minced garlic, salt, and pepper until well combined.

2. Taste and adjust seasoning if needed.

Assembly:

1. Serve the Spinach and Feta Boxty Pancakes warm, topped with a dollop of herb butter.

2. Garnish with extra chopped fresh herbs if desired.

3. Enjoy these contemporary twists on classic Irish boxty pancakes as a delightful appetizer, side dish, or light meal for your St. Patrick's Day celebration!

Tips and Variations:

- **Vegetarian Option:** These pancakes are already vegetarian-friendly. You can make them vegan by using plant-based milk, omitting the egg, and using a vegan feta cheese substitute.

- **Herb Variation:** Feel free to use any combination of your favorite fresh herbs for the herb butter. Basil, cilantro, and tarragon are also excellent choices.

- **Make-Ahead:** You can prepare the pancake batter and herb butter in advance and refrigerate them until ready to use. Simply reheat the pancakes in a skillet before serving and melt the herb butter over them.

- **Side Suggestions:** Serve these Spinach and Feta Boxty Pancakes with Herb Butter alongside a crisp green salad or roasted vegetables for a balanced and flavorful meal.

Roasted Vegetable and Barley Risotto with Parmesan Crisps

Ingredients:
For the risotto:
- 1 cup pearl barley
- 4 cups vegetable broth
- 2 tablespoons olive oil
- 1 onion, finely chopped
- 2 cloves garlic, minced
- 2 carrots, diced
- 1 parsnip, diced
- 1 small butternut squash, peeled, seeded, and diced
- 1 teaspoon dried thyme
- Salt and pepper to taste
- 1/2 cup dry white wine (optional)
- 1/2 cup grated Parmesan cheese
- 2 tablespoons unsalted butter
- 2 tablespoons chopped fresh parsley (for garnish)

For the Parmesan crisps:
- 1 cup grated Parmesan cheese

Instructions:

For the risotto:

1. Preheat your oven to 400°F (200°C).

2. Spread the diced carrots, parsnip, and butternut squash on a baking sheet. Drizzle with olive oil, sprinkle with dried thyme, salt, and pepper, and toss to coat evenly. Roast in the preheated oven for 25-30 minutes, or until the vegetables are tender and lightly caramelized. Set aside.

3. In a large pot, heat olive oil over medium heat. Add the chopped onion and cook until translucent, about 5 minutes. Add the minced garlic and cook for another minute.

4. Add the pearl barley to the pot and toast for 2-3 minutes, stirring frequently.

5. Pour in the dry white wine (if using) and cook until it is absorbed by the barley.

6. Begin adding the vegetable broth to the pot, one cup at a time, stirring frequently and allowing the liquid to be absorbed before adding more. Continue this process until the barley is cooked through and has a creamy consistency, about 30-35 minutes.

7. Once the barley is cooked, stir in the roasted vegetables, grated Parmesan cheese, and butter until well combined. Season with additional salt and pepper to taste if needed.

For the Parmesan crisps:

1. Preheat your oven to 375°F (190°C).

2. Line a baking sheet with parchment paper. Spoon small mounds of grated Parmesan cheese onto the parchment paper, leaving space between each mound.

3. Flatten each mound slightly with the back of a spoon to form thin circles.

4. Bake in the preheated oven for 5-7 minutes, or until the edges are golden brown and crispy.

5. Remove from the oven and let the crisps cool for a few minutes before carefully transferring them to a wire rack to cool completely and become crispy.

Assembly:

1. Serve the Roasted Vegetable and Barley Risotto hot, garnished with chopped fresh parsley and accompanied by Parmesan crisps.

2. Enjoy this contemporary twist on a classic Irish dish as a flavorful and satisfying meal for your St. Patrick's Day celebration!

Tips and Variations:

- **Vegetarian Option:** This dish is already vegetarian-friendly. To make it vegan, simply omit the Parmesan cheese and butter, and use a vegan cheese substitute.

- **Gluten-Free Option:** Substitute the pearl barley with arborio rice or another gluten-free grain for a gluten-free version of this dish.

- **Make-Ahead:** You can roast the vegetables and make the Parmesan crisps ahead of time. The risotto can also be partially prepared in advance and finished just before serving.

- **Side Suggestions:** Serve the Roasted Vegetable and Barley Risotto with a side salad or steamed greens for a complete and balanced meal.

Side Dishes

1. Colcannon with Bacon and Cabbage

2. Roasted Garlic and Thyme Hasselback Potatoes

3. Braised Red Cabbage with Apple and Cranberries

4. Irish Soda Bread with Whipped Butter

5. Boxty Griddle Cakes with Sour Cream and Smoked Salmon

Colcannon with Bacon and Cabbage

Ingredients:
- 4 slices bacon, chopped
- 1 small head cabbage, finely shredded
- 4 cups mashed potatoes (prepared in advance)
- 4 green onions, thinly sliced
- 1/2 cup milk or cream
- Salt and pepper to taste
- 2 tablespoons unsalted butter
- Chopped fresh parsley for garnish

Instructions:

1. In a large skillet, cook the chopped bacon over medium heat until crispy. Remove the bacon from the skillet and set aside, leaving the bacon drippings in the skillet.

2. In the same skillet with the bacon drippings, add the shredded cabbage. Cook, stirring occasionally, until the cabbage is wilted and tender, about 5-7 minutes.

3. In a large pot, combine the mashed potatoes, cooked cabbage, sliced green onions, and crispy bacon.

4. Place the pot over medium heat and pour in the milk or cream. Stir the mixture until everything is well combined and heated through. Add more milk or cream if needed to reach your desired consistency.

5. Season the colcannon with salt and pepper to taste. Stir in the unsalted butter until melted and fully incorporated.

6. Transfer the colcannon to a serving dish and garnish with chopped fresh parsley.

7. Serve the Colcannon with Bacon and Cabbage hot as a comforting and flavorful side dish for your St. Patrick's Day celebration!

Tips and Variations:

- **Vegetarian Option:** Omit the bacon for a vegetarian version of this dish. You can add smoked paprika or liquid smoke to the cabbage for a smoky flavor if desired.

- **Make-Ahead:** You can prepare the mashed potatoes and cook the bacon and cabbage in advance. When ready to serve, reheat the mashed potatoes and cabbage separately before combining them.

- **Herb Variation:** Add chopped fresh herbs such as chives or parsley to the colcannon for extra flavor and freshness.

- **Cheese Addition:** For extra richness, you can stir in shredded cheddar cheese or grated Parmesan cheese into the colcannon before serving.

- **Side Suggestions:** Serve the Colcannon with Bacon and Cabbage alongside traditional Irish dishes such as corned beef and Irish soda bread, or as a side dish to any hearty main course.

Roasted Garlic and Thyme Hasselback Potatoes

Ingredients:
- 4 large russet potatoes, scrubbed clean
- 4 cloves garlic, minced
- 4 tablespoons unsalted butter, melted
- 2 tablespoons olive oil
- 2 tablespoons fresh thyme leaves, chopped
- Salt and pepper to taste
- Chopped fresh parsley for garnish (optional)

Instructions:

1. Preheat your oven to 400°F (200°C). Line a baking sheet with parchment paper.

2. Place a potato on a cutting board, flat side down. Starting from one end, make thin slices along the length of the potato, being careful not to cut all the way through. You want the slices to stay connected at the bottom, creating a "fan" effect. Repeat with the remaining potatoes.

3. In a small bowl, mix together the minced garlic, melted butter, olive oil, and chopped thyme.

4. Place the sliced potatoes on the prepared baking sheet. Brush the garlic and thyme butter mixture generously over each potato, making sure to get some of the mixture in between the slices.

5. Season the potatoes with salt and pepper to taste.

6. Roast the potatoes in the preheated oven for 50-60 minutes, or until the potatoes are golden brown and crispy on the outside, and tender on the inside. You can test for doneness by inserting a fork into the center of a potato – it should slide in easily.

7. Remove the potatoes from the oven and let them cool for a few minutes.

8. Garnish the Roasted Garlic and Thyme Hasselback Potatoes with chopped fresh parsley, if desired, and serve hot.

Tips and Variations:

- **Cheese Addition:** Sprinkle grated Parmesan or cheddar cheese over the potatoes during the last 10 minutes of baking for extra flavor and richness.

- **Herb Variation:** Feel free to experiment with different herbs such as rosemary, sage, or oregano to customize the flavor of the potatoes.

- **Make-Ahead:** You can prepare the potatoes up to the point of brushing them with the garlic and thyme butter mixture. Cover and refrigerate them until ready to bake. Allow them to come to room temperature before roasting.

- **Side Suggestions:** Serve the Roasted Garlic and Thyme Hasselback Potatoes alongside grilled or roasted meats, poultry, or fish, or as a delicious side dish for your St. Patrick's Day feast.

Braised Red Cabbage with Apple and Cranberries

Ingredients:
- 1 medium red cabbage, thinly sliced
- 2 tablespoons olive oil
- 1 large onion, thinly sliced
- 2 apples, peeled, cored, and diced
- 1/2 cup dried cranberries
- 1/4 cup apple cider vinegar
- 1/4 cup maple syrup or honey
- 1/2 teaspoon ground cinnamon
- 1/4 teaspoon ground nutmeg
- Salt and pepper to taste
- 1/2 cup vegetable or chicken broth
- Chopped fresh parsley for garnish (optional)

Instructions:

1. Heat olive oil in a large skillet or Dutch oven over medium heat. Add the thinly sliced onion and cook until softened and translucent, about 5 minutes.

2. Add the thinly sliced red cabbage to the skillet and cook, stirring occasionally, until it starts to wilt, about 5-7 minutes.

3. Stir in the diced apples and dried cranberries, and cook for another 3-4 minutes.

4. Add the apple cider vinegar, maple syrup or honey, ground cinnamon, ground nutmeg, salt, and pepper to the skillet. Stir to combine and coat the cabbage mixture evenly with the seasonings.

5. Pour the vegetable or chicken broth into the skillet and bring the mixture to a simmer.

6. Reduce the heat to low, cover, and let the cabbage mixture simmer gently for about 30-40 minutes, stirring occasionally, until the cabbage is tender and the flavors have melded together.

7. Taste and adjust seasoning with salt and pepper if needed.

8. Once the Braised Red Cabbage with Apple and Cranberries is cooked to your liking, remove it from the heat.

9. Transfer the braised red cabbage to a serving dish and garnish with chopped fresh parsley, if desired.

10. Serve the Braised Red Cabbage with Apple and Cranberries warm as a delightful side dish for your St. Patrick's Day celebration!

Tips and Variations:

- **Make-Ahead:** You can prepare the Braised Red Cabbage with Apple and Cranberries in advance and reheat it gently on the stovetop or in the microwave before serving.

- **Vegetarian and Vegan Options:** This dish is naturally vegetarian and can be made vegan by using maple syrup instead of honey, and vegetable broth instead of chicken broth.

- **Nut Addition:** For added crunch and flavor, you can sprinkle chopped toasted pecans or walnuts over the Braised Red Cabbage with Apple and Cranberries just before serving.

- **Side Suggestions:** Serve this flavorful dish alongside roasted meats, poultry, or tofu, or as a colorful addition to your St. Patrick's Day buffet.

Irish Soda Bread with Whipped Butter

Ingredients:
For the Irish Soda Bread:
- 4 cups all-purpose flour
- 1 tablespoon granulated sugar
- 1 teaspoon baking soda
- 1 teaspoon salt
- 1 3/4 cups buttermilk
- 1/2 cup raisins or currants (optional)
- 1 tablespoon caraway seeds (optional)
- 1 tablespoon melted butter, for brushing (optional)

For the Whipped Butter:
- 1/2 cup unsalted butter, softened
- 1 tablespoon honey or maple syrup
- 1/4 teaspoon salt

Instructions:

For the Irish Soda Bread:

1. Preheat your oven to 425°F (220°C). Lightly grease a baking sheet or line it with parchment paper.

2. In a large mixing bowl, whisk together the all-purpose flour, sugar, baking soda, and salt.

3. If using, stir in the raisins or currants and caraway seeds.

4. Make a well in the center of the dry ingredients and pour in the buttermilk. Using a wooden spoon or your hands, gently mix until a soft dough forms. Be careful not to overmix.

5. Turn the dough out onto a lightly floured surface and shape it into a round loaf. Place the loaf on the prepared baking sheet.

6. Use a sharp knife to make a deep cross-shaped cut on the top of the loaf. This helps the bread to expand while baking.

7. Bake the Irish Soda Bread in the preheated oven for 15 minutes. Then reduce the oven temperature to 400°F (200°C) and continue baking for another 25-30 minutes, or until the bread is golden brown and sounds hollow when tapped on the bottom.

8. Remove the bread from the oven and transfer it to a wire rack to cool slightly. Brush the top of the bread with melted butter, if desired.

For the Whipped Butter:

1. In a mixing bowl, combine the softened butter, honey or maple syrup, and salt.

2. Using a hand mixer or stand mixer fitted with the whisk attachment, beat the mixture on medium-high speed until light and fluffy, about 3-5 minutes.

3. Transfer the whipped butter to a serving dish.

Assembly:

1. Serve slices of the warm Irish Soda Bread with the whipped butter on the side.

2. Enjoy this delicious and comforting bread as a delightful addition to your St. Patrick's Day celebration!

Tips and Variations:
- **Customization:** Feel free to customize the Irish Soda Bread by adding other ingredients such as chopped nuts, dried cranberries, or orange zest for additional flavor and texture.

- **Make-Ahead:** You can bake the Irish Soda Bread in advance and reheat it in the oven just before serving to refresh it.

- **Storage:** Store any leftover Irish Soda Bread in an airtight container at room temperature for up to 2-3 days.

- **Variation:** For a savory twist, omit the sugar and add grated cheese and chopped herbs to the dough.

Boxty Griddle Cakes with Sour Cream and Smoked Salmon

Ingredients:

For the Boxty Griddle Cakes:

- 2 cups grated raw potatoes
- 1 cup all-purpose flour
- 1 teaspoon baking powder
- 1/2 teaspoon salt
- 1/4 teaspoon black pepper
- 1/2 cup milk
- 2 tablespoons unsalted butter, melted
- 1 egg, lightly beaten
- 2 green onions, finely chopped
- 2 tablespoons chopped fresh parsley
- 2 tablespoons vegetable oil (for cooking)

For the Toppings:

- Sour cream
- Smoked salmon slices
- Fresh dill, for garnish
- Lemon wedges, for serving

Instructions:

For the Boxty Griddle Cakes:

1. Place the grated raw potatoes in a clean kitchen towel and squeeze out as much liquid as possible.

2. In a large mixing bowl, combine the grated potatoes, all-purpose flour, baking powder, salt, and black pepper.

3. In a separate bowl, whisk together the milk, melted butter, and beaten egg.

4. Pour the wet ingredients into the dry ingredients and stir until just combined.

5. Fold in the chopped green onions and chopped fresh parsley until evenly distributed throughout the batter.

6. Heat a griddle or large skillet over medium heat and lightly grease it with vegetable oil.

7. Spoon the batter onto the hot griddle to form small pancakes, using about 1/4 cup of batter for each pancake. Use the back of the spoon to spread the batter into a circle.

8. Cook the Boxty Griddle Cakes for 2-3 minutes on each side, or until golden brown and cooked through.

9. Remove the cooked griddle cakes from the griddle and keep them warm while you prepare the toppings.

Assembly:

1. To serve, top each Boxty Griddle Cake with a dollop of sour cream and a slice of smoked salmon.

2. Garnish with fresh dill and serve with lemon wedges on the side.

3. Enjoy these delightful Boxty Griddle Cakes with Sour Cream and Smoked Salmon as an elegant appetizer or light meal for your St. Patrick's Day celebration!

Tips and Variations:

- **Make-Ahead:** You can prepare the Boxty Griddle Cake batter in advance and refrigerate it for up to 24 hours before cooking. Just give it a quick stir before cooking the pancakes.

- **Vegetarian Option:** For a vegetarian version, you can omit the smoked salmon and instead top the griddle cakes with sliced avocado, cherry tomatoes, and a drizzle of balsamic glaze.

- **Gluten-Free Option:** Substitute the all-purpose flour with a gluten-free flour blend to make these griddle cakes gluten-free.

- **Variation:** Feel free to customize the toppings with your favorite ingredients, such as capers, red onion slices, or microgreens.

Desserts

1. Bailey's Irish Cream Chocolate Cheesecake

2. Apple and Blackberry Crumble with Vanilla Custard

3. Guinness Chocolate Cake with Salted Caramel Frosting

4. Shamrock-shaped Shortbread Cookies

5. Irish Coffee Panna Cotta with Whiskey Caramel Sauce

Bailey's Irish Cream Chocolate Cheesecake

Ingredients:

For the Chocolate Crust:

- 1 1/2 cups chocolate cookie crumbs (from about 20 chocolate sandwich cookies)
- 1/4 cup unsalted butter, melted

For the Chocolate Cheesecake Filling:

- 24 ounces (680g) cream cheese, softened
- 1 cup granulated sugar
- 1/4 cup cocoa powder
- 4 large eggs
- 1/2 cup Bailey's Irish Cream liqueur
- 1 teaspoon vanilla extract
- 1 cup semi-sweet chocolate chips, melted and slightly cooled

For the Bailey's Whipped Cream Topping:

- 1 cup heavy cream
- 2 tablespoons powdered sugar
- 2 tablespoons Bailey's Irish Cream liqueur

Instructions:

For the Chocolate Crust:

1. Preheat your oven to 350°F (175°C). Grease a 9-inch springform pan.

2. In a mixing bowl, combine the chocolate cookie crumbs and melted butter. Press the mixture evenly onto the bottom of the prepared springform pan.

3. Bake the crust in the preheated oven for 8-10 minutes. Remove from the oven and let it cool while you prepare the filling.

For the Chocolate Cheesecake Filling:

1. In a large mixing bowl, beat the cream cheese and granulated sugar until smooth and creamy.

2. Add the cocoa powder and beat until well combined.

3. Add the eggs, one at a time, beating well after each addition.

4. Stir in the Bailey's Irish Cream liqueur and vanilla extract until incorporated.

5. Fold in the melted semi-sweet chocolate until evenly distributed throughout the batter.

6. Pour the cheesecake filling over the cooled chocolate crust in the springform pan, spreading it out evenly.

7. Bake the cheesecake in the preheated oven for 45-50 minutes, or until the edges are set but the center is still slightly jiggly.

8. Turn off the oven and leave the cheesecake inside with the oven door slightly ajar for about 1 hour to cool gradually.

9. Remove the cheesecake from the oven and run a knife around the edges to loosen it from the pan. Let it cool completely, then refrigerate for at least 4 hours or overnight to set.

For the Bailey's Whipped Cream Topping:

1. In a mixing bowl, beat the heavy cream until soft peaks form.

2. Add the powdered sugar and Bailey's Irish Cream liqueur, and continue beating until stiff peaks form.

Assembly:

1. Once the cheesecake is chilled and set, spread the Bailey's whipped cream topping over the top.

2. Optionally, garnish with grated chocolate or chocolate shavings.

3. Slice and serve the Bailey's Irish Cream Chocolate Cheesecake chilled.

Tips and Variations:
- **Ganache Topping:** For an extra decadent touch, spread a layer of chocolate ganache over the top of the cheesecake before adding the Bailey's whipped cream topping.

- **Chocolate Drizzle:** Drizzle melted chocolate over the whipped cream topping for a decorative finish.

- **Crust Variation:** You can use crushed chocolate graham crackers or chocolate wafers instead of chocolate sandwich cookies for the crust.

- **Make-Ahead:** The cheesecake can be made a day or two in advance and stored in the refrigerator until ready to serve.

Apple and Blackberry Crumble with Vanilla Custard

Ingredients:
For the Fruit Filling:
- 4 medium apples (such as Granny Smith or Braeburn), peeled, cored, and sliced
- 2 cups fresh or frozen blackberries
- 1/4 cup granulated sugar
- 2 tablespoons all-purpose flour
- 1 teaspoon ground cinnamon
- 1/4 teaspoon ground nutmeg
- Zest of 1 lemon
- Juice of 1/2 lemon

For the Crumble Topping:
- 1 cup all-purpose flour
- 1/2 cup rolled oats
- 1/2 cup granulated sugar
- 1/2 cup unsalted butter, chilled and cubed
- 1/4 teaspoon salt

For the Vanilla Custard:
- 2 cups whole milk
- 1/2 cup granulated sugar
- 4 large egg yolks
- 2 tablespoons cornstarch
- 1 teaspoon vanilla extract

Instructions:
For the Fruit Filling:
1. Preheat your oven to 375°F (190°C). Grease a 9x13-inch baking dish or individual ramekins.
2. In a large mixing bowl, combine the sliced apples, blackberries, granulated sugar, all-purpose flour, ground cinnamon, ground nutmeg, lemon zest, and lemon juice. Toss until the fruit is evenly coated.
3. Transfer the fruit mixture to the prepared baking dish or ramekins, spreading it out evenly.

For the Crumble Topping:
1. In a separate mixing bowl, combine the all-purpose flour, rolled oats, granulated sugar, and salt.
2. Add the chilled cubed butter to the dry ingredients. Using your fingertips or a pastry cutter, work the butter into the flour mixture until it resembles coarse crumbs.
3. Sprinkle the crumble topping evenly over the fruit filling in the baking dish or ramekins.
4. Place the baking dish or ramekins on a baking sheet to catch any drips, and bake in the preheated oven for 30-35 minutes, or until the fruit is bubbling and the crumble topping is golden brown.
5. Remove from the oven and let it cool for a few minutes before serving.

For the Vanilla Custard:
1. In a saucepan, heat the whole milk over medium heat until it begins to simmer. Remove from heat and set aside.
2. In a mixing bowl, whisk together the granulated sugar, egg yolks, and cornstarch until well combined and slightly pale in color.
3. Slowly pour the hot milk into the egg mixture, whisking constantly to temper the eggs.

4. Return the mixture to the saucepan and place it over medium heat. Cook, stirring constantly, until the custard thickens and coats the back of a spoon.

5. Remove from heat and stir in the vanilla extract.

Assembly:

1. Serve the warm Apple and Blackberry Crumble with a generous spoonful of vanilla custard.

2. Enjoy this delightful and comforting dessert as the perfect ending to your St. Patrick's Day celebration!

Tips and Variations:

- **Ice Cream Topping:** Instead of vanilla custard, serve the Apple and Blackberry Crumble with a scoop of vanilla ice cream for a cold and creamy contrast.

- **Nutty Crunch:** Add chopped nuts such as almonds, pecans, or walnuts to the crumble topping for extra texture and flavor.

- **Seasonal Variation:** Feel free to substitute the blackberries with other seasonal berries such as raspberries, blueberries, or strawberries.

- **Gluten-Free Option:** Use gluten-free flour and certified gluten-free oats to make this recipe gluten-free.

Guinness Chocolate Cake with Salted Caramel Frosting

Ingredients:
For the Guinness Chocolate Cake:
- 1 cup Guinness stout
- 1 cup unsalted butter
- 3/4 cup unsweetened cocoa powder
- 2 cups all-purpose flour
- 2 cups granulated sugar
- 1 1/2 teaspoons baking soda
- 3/4 teaspoon salt
- 2 large eggs
- 2/3 cup sour cream
- 1 teaspoon vanilla extract

For the Salted Caramel Frosting:
- 1 cup granulated sugar
- 6 tablespoons unsalted butter
- 1/2 cup heavy cream
- 1/2 teaspoon salt
- 2 cups powdered sugar, sifted

Instructions:

For the Guinness Chocolate Cake:

1. Preheat your oven to 350°F (175°C). Grease and flour two 9-inch round cake pans.

2. In a saucepan, heat the Guinness and unsalted butter over medium heat until the butter melts. Remove from heat and whisk in the cocoa powder until smooth. Set aside to cool slightly.

3. In a large mixing bowl, whisk together the flour, granulated sugar, baking soda, and salt.

4. In another bowl, beat the eggs, sour cream, and vanilla extract until well combined.

5. Gradually pour the Guinness mixture into the egg mixture, whisking constantly.

6. Add the wet ingredients to the dry ingredients and whisk until just combined and no lumps remain.

7. Divide the batter evenly between the prepared cake pans.

8. Bake in the preheated oven for 35-40 minutes, or until a toothpick inserted into the center of the cakes comes out clean.

9. Remove the cakes from the oven and let them cool in the pans for 10 minutes before transferring them to wire racks to cool completely.

For the Salted Caramel Frosting:

1. In a saucepan, heat the granulated sugar over medium heat, stirring constantly with a wooden spoon until it melts and turns amber in color.

2. Add the unsalted butter and stir until melted and well combined.

3. Slowly pour in the heavy cream while stirring constantly. Be careful, as the mixture will bubble up.

4. Remove the saucepan from the heat and stir in the salt. Let the caramel cool to room temperature.

5. In a mixing bowl, beat the cooled caramel with the powdered sugar until smooth and creamy.

Assembly:

1. Place one cake layer on a serving plate or cake stand. Spread a layer of salted caramel frosting over the top.

2. Place the second cake layer on top and frost the top and sides of the cake with the remaining frosting.

3. Optional: Drizzle additional salted caramel sauce over the top of the cake for extra flavor and decoration.

4. Serve and enjoy this decadent Guinness Chocolate Cake with Salted Caramel Frosting as a delicious centerpiece for your St. Patrick's Day celebration!

Tips and Variations:

- **Make-Ahead:** You can bake the cake layers in advance and freeze them until ready to assemble. The frosting can also be made ahead and stored in the refrigerator. Just bring it to room temperature and re-whip before using.

- **Garnish:** Sprinkle the top of the cake with flaky sea salt or chocolate shavings for added texture and visual appeal.

- **Storage:** Store any leftover cake in an airtight container in the refrigerator for up to 3-4 days.

Shamrock-shaped Shortbread Cookies

Ingredients:
- 1 cup (2 sticks) unsalted butter, softened
- 1/2 cup granulated sugar
- 2 cups all-purpose flour
- 1/4 teaspoon salt
- 1 teaspoon vanilla extract
- Green food coloring (gel or liquid), as needed
- Shamrock-shaped cookie cutter

Instructions:

1. Preheat your oven to 325°F (160°C). Line a baking sheet with parchment paper.

2. In a large mixing bowl, cream together the softened butter and granulated sugar until light and fluffy.

3. Add the vanilla extract and mix until well combined.

4. Gradually add the flour and salt to the butter mixture, mixing until a dough forms. The dough should come together and be smooth.

5. If desired, add a few drops of green food coloring to the dough and mix until evenly colored. Adjust the amount of food coloring according to your preference for shade of green.

6. On a lightly floured surface, roll out the dough to about 1/4 inch thickness.

7. Use the shamrock-shaped cookie cutter to cut out cookies from the dough. Place the cut-out cookies onto the prepared baking sheet, spacing them slightly apart.

8. Gather the scraps of dough, reroll, and cut out more cookies until all the dough is used.

9. Optionally, use a toothpick to create small indents on the surface of each cookie to resemble the veins of a shamrock leaf.

10. Bake the cookies in the preheated oven for 12-15 minutes, or until the edges are lightly golden.

11. Remove the cookies from the oven and let them cool on the baking sheet for a few minutes before transferring them to a wire rack to cool completely.

12. Once cooled, store the Shamrock-shaped Shortbread Cookies in an airtight container at room temperature.

Tips and Variations:
- **Decorate:** If desired, you can decorate the cookies with royal icing, green sugar sprinkles, or edible glitter for added festive flair.

- **Flavor Variation:** Add a hint of citrus zest (such as lemon or lime) to the dough for a refreshing twist on the classic shortbread flavor.

- **Serve:** These cookies are perfect for serving at St. Patrick's Day parties, as gifts, or for enjoying with a cup of tea or coffee.

- **Make-Ahead:** You can prepare the dough in advance and refrigerate it for up to 2 days before baking. Alternatively, you can freeze the unbaked cookie dough for up to 3 months. Simply thaw in the refrigerator before rolling and cutting out the cookies.

Irish Coffee Panna Cotta with Whiskey Caramel Sauce

Ingredients:
For the Irish Coffee Panna Cotta:
- 2 cups heavy cream
- 1/2 cup whole milk
- 1/4 cup granulated sugar
- 2 teaspoons instant coffee granules
- 2 tablespoons Irish whiskey
- 2 teaspoons gelatin powder
- 2 tablespoons cold water

For the Whiskey Caramel Sauce:
- 1 cup granulated sugar
- 1/4 cup water
- 1/2 cup heavy cream
- 2 tablespoons unsalted butter
- 2 tablespoons Irish whiskey
- Pinch of salt

Instructions:

For the Irish Coffee Panna Cotta:

1. In a small bowl, sprinkle the gelatin powder over the cold water and let it bloom for about 5 minutes.

2. In a saucepan, heat the heavy cream, whole milk, granulated sugar, and instant coffee granules over medium heat, stirring occasionally, until the mixture just begins to simmer. Do not let it boil.

3. Remove the saucepan from the heat and stir in the Irish whiskey until well combined.

4. Add the bloomed gelatin mixture to the warm cream mixture, stirring until the gelatin is completely dissolved.

5. Strain the mixture through a fine-mesh sieve to remove any lumps or coffee granules.

6. Divide the mixture evenly among six serving glasses or ramekins. Cover with plastic wrap and refrigerate for at least 4 hours, or until set.

For the Whiskey Caramel Sauce:

1. In a saucepan, combine the granulated sugar and water over medium heat. Cook, swirling the pan occasionally, until the sugar dissolves and the mixture turns a deep amber color.

2. Remove the saucepan from the heat and carefully whisk in the heavy cream. Be cautious, as the mixture will bubble up.

3. Return the saucepan to low heat and stir in the unsalted butter, Irish whiskey, and a pinch of salt. Cook, stirring constantly, until the sauce is smooth and slightly thickened.

4. Remove the sauce from the heat and let it cool slightly before serving.

Assembly:

1. Once the Irish Coffee Panna Cotta has set, spoon a generous amount of the Whiskey Caramel Sauce over each serving.

2. Optionally, garnish with a dollop of whipped cream and a sprinkle of cocoa powder or chocolate shavings.

3. Serve chilled and enjoy this luxurious Irish Coffee Panna Cotta with Whiskey Caramel Sauce as a decadent dessert for your St. Patrick's Day celebration!

Tips and Variations:

- **Make-Ahead:** Both the Irish Coffee Panna Cotta and Whiskey Caramel Sauce can be made a day in advance and stored separately in the refrigerator. Simply assemble the dessert just before serving.

- **Non-Alcoholic Option:** If you prefer not to use alcohol, you can omit the Irish whiskey from both the panna cotta and caramel sauce recipes. Instead, you can add a splash of vanilla extract for flavor.

- **Serve with Coffee:** Accompany this dessert with a freshly brewed cup of Irish coffee for an extra special treat.

- **Variation:** For an added layer of flavor, sprinkle a small amount of finely ground espresso beans over the panna cotta just before serving.

Drinks

1. Classic Irish Coffee with Whipped Cream

2. Black Velvet Cocktail (Guinness and Champagne)

3. Celtic Mule (Irish whiskey, ginger beer, lime)

4. Shamrock Shake (Mint ice cream, milk, whipped cream)

5. Irish Hot Chocolate with Bailey's and Marshmallows

Classic Irish Coffee with Whipped Cream

Ingredients:

- 1 cup freshly brewed hot coffee
- 1 1/2 oz Irish whiskey
- 1 tablespoon brown sugar (adjust to taste)
- Whipped cream (homemade or store-bought)
- Ground nutmeg or cinnamon, for garnish (optional)

Instructions:

1. Brew a cup of your favorite coffee using your preferred method. Make sure it's hot and ready to serve.

2. While the coffee is brewing, warm your glassware by filling it with hot water for a minute or two. Then, discard the water.

3. Pour the hot coffee into the warmed glass until it's about 3/4 full.

4. Add the brown sugar to the coffee and stir until it's completely dissolved.

5. Measure out the Irish whiskey and pour it into the coffee, stirring gently to combine.

6. Top the Irish coffee with a generous dollop of whipped cream. You can either spoon it on top or use a piping bag to create a decorative swirl.

7. Optionally, sprinkle a pinch of ground nutmeg or cinnamon over the whipped cream for extra flavor and presentation.

8. Serve immediately and enjoy your delightful Classic Irish Coffee with Whipped Cream!

Tips and Variations:

- **Whipped Cream:** For homemade whipped cream, simply whip cold heavy cream with a little powdered sugar until it reaches stiff peaks. You can add a splash of vanilla extract for flavor if desired.

- **Sweetness:** Adjust the amount of brown sugar to suit your taste preferences. Some prefer their Irish coffee sweeter, while others prefer it less sweet.

- **Whiskey Choice:** While Irish whiskey is traditional for Irish coffee, you can experiment with different types of whiskey or even flavored liqueurs for unique variations.

- **Garnish Options:** In addition to nutmeg or cinnamon, you can also garnish your Irish coffee with chocolate shavings, cocoa powder, or coffee beans for added flair.

- **Non-Alcoholic Option:** If you prefer a non-alcoholic version, simply omit the whiskey and enjoy a delicious Irish-style coffee with whipped cream.

Black Velvet Cocktail

Ingredients:
- 1 part Guinness stout, chilled
- 1 part Champagne or sparkling wine, chilled
- Lemon twist or edible gold flakes, for garnish (optional)

Instructions:

1. Start by chilling both the Guinness stout and Champagne in the refrigerator for at least a few hours before serving. It's essential to ensure they are cold to maintain their carbonation.

2. Once chilled, carefully pour the Guinness stout into a Champagne flute or tall glass, filling it halfway.

3. Gently pour the Champagne over the back of a spoon onto the Guinness stout, allowing it to float on top and create the distinctive layered effect. The Champagne should fill the remainder of the glass.

4. Optionally, garnish the Black Velvet Cocktail with a twist of lemon zest for a bright citrus aroma or sprinkle with edible gold flakes for a touch of elegance.

5. Serve immediately and enjoy your sophisticated Black Velvet Cocktail as a delightful and unique beverage to celebrate St. Patrick's Day!

Tips and Variations:

- **Proper Pouring Technique:** To achieve the layered effect, pour the Champagne slowly and gently over the Guinness stout using the back of a spoon. This helps to create a clear separation between the two liquids.

- **Champagne Alternatives:** If you prefer, you can use other sparkling wines or prosecco instead of Champagne. Choose a dry or brut variety to complement the richness of the Guinness.

- **Experiment with Flavors:** For a twist on the traditional recipe, you can add a splash of flavored liqueur such as Chambord (raspberry), Cointreau (orange), or Crème de Cassis (blackcurrant) to enhance the flavor profile of the cocktail.

- **Non-Alcoholic Version:** For a non-alcoholic alternative, you can substitute the Champagne with sparkling apple cider or ginger ale for a refreshing mocktail version of the Black Velvet Cocktail.

- **Presentation:** Serve the Black Velvet Cocktail in tall, slender glasses to showcase the beautiful layers and visually stunning contrast between the dark Guinness and golden Champagne.

Celtic Mule

Ingredients:
- 2 ounces Irish whiskey
- 4 ounces ginger beer
- 1/2 ounce fresh lime juice
- Lime wedge, for garnish
- Crystallized ginger or fresh ginger slices, for garnish (optional)
- Ice cubes

Instructions:

1. Fill a copper mug or highball glass with ice cubes.

2. Pour the Irish whiskey and fresh lime juice over the ice.

3. Top up the glass with ginger beer, leaving some room for garnish.

4. Give the cocktail a gentle stir to mix the ingredients.

5. Garnish with a lime wedge and a piece of crystallized ginger or fresh ginger slices, if desired, for an extra pop of flavor and visual appeal.

6. Serve immediately and enjoy your refreshing Celtic Mule as a delightful cocktail to celebrate St. Patrick's Day!

Tips and Variations:

- **Whiskey Choices:** Experiment with different types of Irish whiskey to find your favorite flavor profile. Whether you prefer a smooth and mellow whiskey or one with more robust and complex notes, there's a whiskey out there to suit your taste.

- **Ginger Beer Selection:** Opt for a high-quality ginger beer with a balanced blend of sweetness and spice to complement the Irish whiskey and lime juice. Look for brands that use natural ingredients and have a bold ginger flavor.

- **Fresh Lime Juice:** For the best flavor, use freshly squeezed lime juice rather than bottled lime juice. It adds a bright and zesty citrus element to the cocktail, balancing the richness of the whiskey and the spiciness of the ginger beer.

- **Garnish Ideas:** Get creative with your garnishes! In addition to lime wedges and crystallized ginger, you can also add a sprig of fresh mint or a twist of lime zest for a burst of color and aroma.

- **Mocktail Version:** For a non-alcoholic version of the Celtic Mule, simply omit the Irish whiskey and replace it with an equal amount of extra ginger beer. You'll still get the refreshing combination of spicy ginger and tangy lime without the alcohol.

- **Presentation:** Serve the Celtic Mule in a copper mug or a highball glass for an authentic and stylish presentation. The copper mug not only looks elegant but also helps to keep the cocktail cold and refreshing.

Contemporary Shamrock Shake

Ingredients:
For the Shamrock Shake:
- 2 cups mint chocolate chip ice cream (or plain mint ice cream)
- 1 cup whole milk
- 1/2 teaspoon pure vanilla extract
- Green food coloring (optional)
- Whipped cream, for topping
- Maraschino cherries or mint leaves, for garnish (optional)

For the Whipped Cream:
- 1 cup heavy cream, chilled
- 2 tablespoons powdered sugar
- 1/2 teaspoon pure vanilla extract

Instructions:

For the Shamrock Shake:

1. In a blender, combine the mint chocolate chip ice cream, whole milk, and pure vanilla extract. If desired, add a few drops of green food coloring for a vibrant green color.

2. Blend the ingredients until smooth and creamy, ensuring that the ice cream is fully incorporated into the milk.

3. Taste the Shamrock Shake and adjust the sweetness or mint flavoring as desired.

4. Pour the Shamrock Shake into serving glasses, leaving some room at the top for whipped cream.

For the Whipped Cream:

1. In a mixing bowl, combine the chilled heavy cream, powdered sugar, and pure vanilla extract.

2. Using a hand mixer or stand mixer fitted with the whisk attachment, whip the cream on medium-high speed until stiff peaks form. Be careful not to overwhip.

3. Spoon or pipe the whipped cream onto the top of each Shamrock Shake.

Assembly:

1. Top each Shamrock Shake with a dollop of whipped cream.

2. Optionally, garnish with a maraschino cherry or a sprig of fresh mint for a festive touch.

3. Serve immediately and enjoy your contemporary Shamrock Shake as a delightful and refreshing treat for St. Patrick's Day!

Tips and Variations:

- **Customize the Mint Flavor:** If you prefer a stronger mint flavor, you can add a drop or two of pure peppermint extract to the Shamrock Shake mixture before blending.

- **Texture Variation:** For added texture and crunch, sprinkle crushed chocolate cookies or chocolate shavings over the whipped cream topping.

- **Alcoholic Version:** For an adult twist, you can add a splash of Irish cream liqueur or crème de menthe to the Shamrock Shake mixture before blending.

- **Non-Dairy Option:** Use your favorite non-dairy mint ice cream and dairy-free whipped cream alternatives to make a vegan-friendly version of the Shamrock Shake.

- **Make-Ahead:** You can prepare the Shamrock Shake mixture and whipped cream in advance and assemble the shakes just before serving to ensure they're fresh and cold.

Irish Hot Chocolate with Bailey's and Marshmallows

Ingredients:
- 2 cups whole milk
- 1/2 cup heavy cream
- 4 ounces semisweet or dark chocolate, chopped
- 2 tablespoons unsweetened cocoa powder
- 2 tablespoons granulated sugar (adjust to taste)
- 1/4 teaspoon pure vanilla extract
- 1/4 cup Bailey's Irish Cream (or to taste)
- Whipped cream, for topping
- Mini marshmallows, for garnish
- Chocolate shavings or cocoa powder, for garnish (optional)

Instructions:

1. In a saucepan, combine the whole milk and heavy cream. Heat over medium-low heat until it begins to simmer, but do not boil.

2. Add the chopped chocolate, cocoa powder, and granulated sugar to the saucepan. Whisk continuously until the chocolate is completely melted and the mixture is smooth and creamy.

3. Stir in the pure vanilla extract and Bailey's Irish Cream until well combined. Taste the hot chocolate and adjust the sweetness or Bailey's amount according to your preference.

4. Once the hot chocolate is heated through and well combined, remove the saucepan from the heat.

5. Pour the Irish hot chocolate into serving mugs.

6. Top each mug of Irish hot chocolate with a generous dollop of whipped cream.

7. Garnish with mini marshmallows, chocolate shavings, or a dusting of cocoa powder, if desired.

8. Serve immediately and enjoy your cozy Irish Hot Chocolate with Bailey's and Marshmallows as a delightful St. Patrick's Day treat!

Tips and Variations:

- **Alcoholic Strength:** Adjust the amount of Bailey's Irish Cream to suit your taste preferences. You can add more or less depending on how strong you'd like the alcoholic flavor to be.

- **Whipped Cream Variations:** Get creative with your whipped cream topping by adding a splash of Bailey's or a sprinkle of cinnamon or nutmeg for extra flavor.

- **Marshmallow Options:** If you prefer, you can use regular-sized marshmallows instead of mini marshmallows. You can also toast the marshmallows under the broiler or with a kitchen torch for a fun and gooey twist.

- **Dairy-Free Option:** Substitute the whole milk and heavy cream with your favorite non-dairy alternatives such as almond milk or coconut milk for a dairy-free version of Irish hot chocolate.

- **Make-Ahead:** You can prepare the hot chocolate mixture in advance and reheat it gently on the stove or in the microwave when ready to serve. Add the Bailey's just before serving to preserve its flavor.